A Family
Possessed

L. W. Stevenson

Mayhaven Publishing

Mayhaven Publishing

P O Box 557
Mahomet, IL 61853
USA

Cover Art & Design by Cullen J. Porter

First Edition—First Printing 2000 1 2 3 4 5 6 7 8 9 10

Library of Congress Number: 99-075131
ISBN: 1-878044-63-X

Dedication

This book is dedicated to our daughter,
Mrs. W. C. (Saralee) Griffith

iv...

Table of Contents

Introduction

Background description, settings and characters set the mood for a well-told tale. A believable story includes predictable characters and events. For example, a spectral visitor would ordinarily be expected to materialize in a setting associated with supernatural happenings. An abandoned house with shattered windows, a weed-choked yard lend credibility to a tale of unhappy spirits. The most pragmatic mind can visualize a presence waiting at the top of a creaking stairway or behind a sagging door.

That is one of the reasons it's difficult to relate this story as it was told to me. The characters and setting don't fit into the expected pattern for such a tale.

One of the narrators, Robert, owns a retail store that supplies feed, grain and fertilizer to area farmers. He is also a part-time farmer and cattleman. He is a friendly, out-going man with a reputation for honesty. When we spoke, he had not missed a church service or Bible class for over a quarter century.

Becky, Robert's wife, is a gentle, pretty woman who is well acquainted with housework, gardening, canning and even dirt farming. She is a professional seamstress and an accomplished artist. One would never imagine her concocting a bizarre story just to shock others or to call attention to herself.

Robert and Becky have four children, two boys and two girls. Family ties are so strong and mutual affection so evident that it is almost embarrassing to write of the animosity that developed violent confrontations that occurred. The eldest son is still reluctant to discuss the times he shouted at his mother and frightened his sisters with his strange, uncharacteristic behavior.

The other principal character is a devout protestant minister, an ex-marine standing over six feet tall and weighing in excess of two hundred pounds, who was frightened to childish tears by his experience. A minister so unacquainted with exorcism that he forgot to bring his Bible when he was called by the terrified family.

I was asked to collaborate on a story peopled with out-of-place characters in an unlikely setting. I was not asked to explain it or to even believe it, but to tell it as they experienced it. The family and the minister recorded those experiences and I spent many hours listening to the tapes and transcribing them, verifying dates and details and personal impressions.

The events took place over a period of two decades. Portions of those years passed uneventfully. Other portions were crowded with unexplained happenings.

It was not until the later years that the happenings became frightening. It now seems unbelievable that when it all began the family was intrigued and amused. The girls found a rapt audience at school when they told of the strange occurrences in their home. Later the family banded together in silence, fearing ridicule.

That is why they tell their story at this late date. Others to whom similar things are happening may feel a sense of helplessness. Robert now feels that if he had asked for assistance when it began there would not have been such a long time of feeling alone with their problems. Many of us believe in life after death but we are not prepared to believe that the living and the dead occasionally cross paths.

Do I believe what I was told? I believe the family members are completely honest in describing what they saw and heard. I am certain of the integrity of each person.

Perhaps the minister said it best when he recorded: "I do not believe and shall never believe in ghosts, goblins or witches, but I do believe in the existence of good and evil. That family and myself were in the presence of something evil."

As for myself, I believe in psychic phenomena to the extent that when I was asked to write this factual account, I listened to the tapes in the rooms where it all took place. I was advised by a minister friend that if I felt a sense of uneasiness I should not write the story. I felt nothing but an interest in what was being told. I stood under the big maple tree where the tortured dogs once swung and felt nothing but revulsion that such an evil thing could happen. I stood in the basement storage room where the exorcist was freezing cold and nauseated. I petted the dog, blinded, perhaps, by some malevolent spirit and felt only compassion for the unfortunate creature.

And yet there were times when I sat alone in my study and listened to the tapes that I confess to a sense of uneasiness. There are shadowed corners in my basement office and creaks and sounds of the house became unnerving.

At those times, I switched off the tape recorder, unplugged my typewriter and went upstairs into the daylight.

Chapter 1

My involvement in the family's experiences began at a family reunion in a city park.

I had read a recent article in an area newspaper which described the trials of a rural family who were firmly convinced that their home was possessed by supernatural beings. Like most feature articles, it was quickly read and forgotten. Since the family wished to remain anonymous, I had no idea that I would become personally involved in their problems. I certainly never connected the story with any member of mine or my wife's family.

It was the annual gathering of my wife's side of the family, attended by near and distant relatives, most of whom we would not see again until the next reunion or funeral.

I am fond of my wife's family and respect their history and

considerable achievements. One of my favorite cousins is one whom I shall call Robert. Robert is an articulate man who usually has a great deal to say about a variety of topics, but what he says usually makes sense and is always interesting. He has as much sincere enthusiasm as any person I have ever met. When he shakes your hand and says, "Good morning. It's good to see you," you have a warm feeling that it is a very good morning, indeed, and that seeing you may well be the highlight of Robert's day. He seems an unlikely candidate for demoniac possession.

It was a warm, beautiful Sunday. I had shaken many hands and assured many relatives of my good health and busy schedule. I went and sat on a park bench outside the crowded pavilion where the picnic lunch was spread. I had decided to absorb the sunshine and beauty of the day. Laughter and conversation and the shouts of children flowed around me. It was a good place to be and a good time to be there.

Robert cannot abide a lonely person, which I wasn't. I was alone but not lonely. Seeing me sitting by myself, though, he made his way through aunts and uncles and sat beside me.

After exchanges on health and business and other topics, I told him, "You and Becky have a beautiful home on the farm you bought. You must be very happy."

"Yes," he said, "we've worked hard on it, all of us. We should be happy." He was serious, almost somber, totally out of character. He stared across the park with its huge oaks and hickories.

"Steve," he said, "I'm going to tell you something. You wouldn't believe the hell we've been through on that place."

Thinking of financial or family problems, I didn't question him. If he wanted me to know, he'd tell me. He clasped his hands across his knees and looked at me.

"Steve," he said, settling down beside me, "we've had ghosts in that house. I know you probably think I'm off my rocker, but we've seen them. We've had unbelievable experiences and it's been going on for years. We've even asked for help from psychics. Can you imagine that?"

He seemed to expect some sort of reaction. "Tell me," he said, "do you believe in ghosts?"

"I've heard of strange happenings," I said, "but I was never sure of what was factual and what was imagination."

"Well, at least you're not laughing. Believe me, we've had our share of that. But, I'm serious. Our lives have been affected by it." He stood up and smiled at me. He was Robert again.

"Would you like to hear the whole story? We owe you folks a visit anyway. I'd like to share it with you. Even if you don't believe it, you'll find it interesting." I told him we'd look forward to a visit and he went back to the pavilion.

Going home from the reunion, I told my wife about my conversation with Robert.

"What do you suppose they saw?" I said, "I don't know what's happened, but whatever it was, he's deeply troubled. I hope they do visit. I'd like to hear what they have to say."

Two weeks later, on Sunday afternoon, Robert called. If we were not busy that evening, he and Becky would drive up for a visit. I told him to come ahead; we'd be delighted.

My wife popped popcorn and when Robert and Becky arrived shortly after dark, we sat at the kitchen table and snacked and drank coffee. We talked of family happenings and after awhile we went into the living room and settled into comfortable chairs.

"Tell me about your ghosts," I said.

"First," he said, "you must understand that what I tell you happened to us over a long period of time, several years. The first incidents were right after we built the new house. The last, the frightening ones, happened during the last few months. That's when we asked for help."

"Weren't you and the children frightened during those years? Why would you live with ghosts in the house all that time?"

"We never thought seriously about ghosts in the beginning, until it finally became obvious that was the only explanation for the things that were happening to us."

"Why didn't you sell the place and move?"

"What reason would I give for selling out, that there were ghosts in the house? Besides, I had always thought, as you said at the reunion, that ghosts were products of a vivid imagination. Anyway, most of the events were not frightening at first. Some of them were even funny.

"We rationalized, as anyone would have done. Let me give some examples. Suppose you are sitting in this living room and you hear what sounds like footsteps in the basement. You go to the basement and there's no one there. What would you think?"

"I'd think it was an outside noise that sounded like it came from the house. You mean, would I think it was a supernatural happening? No."

"Exactly. Suppose that right now we hear a knock at that door. We both hear it. Distinctly. You go to the door and there's no one there. How would you explain the knock?"

"I'd probably think it was some noise outside that sounded like a knock on the door."

Right. Now, suppose you get up during the night to go to the bathroom and you see the shadow of a person standing right there, in the corner of this room. In the half light it looks as though there is someone standing there, not moving, not threatening. Just standing there. What would you do?"

"I'd probably be startled at first and then I'd realize I'd seen the shadow of some object in this room."

"You see? Those were the kind of things that happened at first. Startling at times, but nothing to lose sleep over. Looking back over that period of time, we realize now that was only the beginning. They were not merely puzzling events. They were building to the point that, for awhile, we lived in real fear. If we'd known then what we know now, we'd have contacted professional help long before we did."

"Are you still troubled by whatever you saw?"

"You really mean by whatever we *think* we saw or felt, don't you? We're used to that attitude. We've been told more than once that it's all in our minds. But when six minds all think the same thoughts and see and hear the same things, it must be more that imagination. As for our troubles now, that's a different story. Let me start at the beginning and tell you about it."

"Why are you telling me the story?"

"For several reasons. First, we want an organized account of our experiences. You're a writer, the only writer we know and we think you can put it together in an organized way.

"Second, we think it should be told. We've learned that there are many other families that are troubled by incidents like ours. Sometimes they talk about it, but more often they don't. We know of families that have moved out of their homes because they were unable to explain some things that happened, except that they were supernatural. Most people are reluctant to talk about their experiences. People do laugh you know. Some of our relatives joke about it. They'll never believe how real it was, that we're not making it up or at least taking some coincidences and adding a dash of imagination. I don't suppose I would believe it myself if it hadn't happened to us.

"Steve, this is important to us. We want people to know that such things really do happen and we especially want them to know that if and when they do happen, they don't have to live with it. If our story helps just one person, it'll be worth it."

"Have you considered what will happen to you and your family if your story becomes public knowledge? You'll have more curiosity seekers than you can handle. Few people will admit that they believe in haunted houses, but almost everyone would like to see one."

"We've discussed that for hours. Can we tell it and remain anonymous? That's how we'd like it."

"First let me hear it. All the way through."

Chapter 2

Robert and Becky had a long-standing dream of buying a farm of their own and when at last the time came when they could afford at least a substantial down payment, they asked Robert's father, John, to assist them in a search for a small livestock and grain farm. Robert and his father spent several weeks reading real estate listings, attending farm sales and tracking down possible locations.

One night John called to say that he had been told of a farm for sale that according to the description might be the place they had been looking for. Robert recalled passing the property several times. He remembered the farm's run-down appearance and was wondering why it had been allowed to fall into such a sorry state.

The day after John's call, he and Robert drove to the farmstead. It was a hundred-acre tract consisting of poor soil, a multitude of blackberry bushes and a parcel of pasture overgrown with weeds. A thickly-wooded area of perhaps twenty acres is at the southwest edge of the property. A shallow, spring-fed ditch traverses east to west, south of a barn. There was a ramshackled, four-room house, and the weathered barn was perilously leaning just a few yards west of the house. An abandoned well partially filled with bricks and trash was at the southwest corner of the house. There was another well a few yards west of the house. The lane leading to the house from a graveled road, a sloping distance of a couple hundred feet, was merely well-tracked clay soil, obviously impassable in inclement weather.

An elderly widow, a Mrs. Nancy Blake, had lived there alone for many years. When she died, the property was left to a daughter who lived in a nearby town.

There was a tenant family living in the house, but they had done little to improve the yard or buildings. The yard was unmowed and the garden needed weeding. The house was weatherboard, faded to a drab, gray color.

For one with less love for land and livestock, reclaiming the place would have seemed an impossible task. But it was reasonably priced, it was not far from a good school, and it was near a small community and only a few miles from two larger towns.

Best of all, Robert would not have to depend on the farm for an income while he was building it into a paying proposition. He was employed at the farm supply store which he would later purchase.

One evening, shortly before dark, Robert and John took their wives to see the farm. Becky had been forewarned that it was not the place they had dreamed of, but she was appalled at the work that would have to be done if they bought it. Robert excitedly pointed out the good points and glossed over the bad ones. She tried to see it through his eyes and since she loved Robert, she told him she loved the farm.

The tenant's wife asked Becky and Ruth, John's wife, inside while her husband visited with John and Robert. The structure would have to be demolished to make way for a new house, but Robert thought there might be lumber worth salvaging. The tenant knew little about the house's construction except that it had been built around a one-room building that had been dragged in from a neighboring farm many years before.

The house was no more pretentious inside than out. Four rooms, two small closets. Papered walls that evidently had never been cleaned. Brown, stained ceiling spots indicating roof leakage. Worn, kitchen linoleum. Soiled, frill lace curtains and dark green window blinds. No running water. No bathroom or sink. Just two galvanized water buckets and a granite-colored dish pan on the cabinet.

It wasn't difficult to visualize a little old lady living out her last years in such a place. No doubt, in the beginning, it would be no worse or better than other farm homes in the area. Rural electrification and improved road repair and maintenance dramatically changed the life style of rural residents except for those who, like Mrs. Blake, stayed with the old way of life.

The three women sat at the oil-cloth covered kitchen table and chatted about canning and cooking. Becky described the floor plan of the new house and although she would never know the life style Becky was describing, the tenant's wife seemed genuinely interested and repeatedly remarked how lovely the new home would be and how happy the children would be, growing up in the country.

Becky asked her if she knew Mrs. Blake well.

"As much as I cared to know her. She was not what you'd call a friendly person. I reckon my husband knew her as well as anybody. He farmed for her and did her shopping. She didn't leave the place very often. She was a little odd, but she was a hard worker some years back. She had to be to raise her daughter on this place after her husband died. He died there in that bedroom. You might not think so, looking at it now, but she put in a lot of hard work on this place. It was the only thing she had left, except her daughter, of course.

There was an awkward pause in the conversation and the tenant's wife asked, "Have you and your husband been told about the ghost?"

"A ghost? No we haven't. Who is it? Who's it suppose to be the ghost of?"

"I wouldn't know about that, but I have my ideas. There is one, though. My daughter and I have seen her. She comes across the barn yard and stands under that big maple tree, after dark."

That night Becky asked Robert if he had heard about the ghost. He said he thought a ghost was supposed to return to the place it loved in life and he didn't see how anyone could love that old run down house enough to come back to it.

Chapter 3

There was little worth salvaging in the house and as soon as the tenants moved, Robert began to tear it down. Bulldozers were trucked in to root out shrubs and blackberry bushes and excavate a basement. Bulldozers always attract an audience and Robert's neighbors came to watch them dig and scoop. Several remarked that they were pleased to see the changes taking place. The old house had long been a community eyesore.

One of the neighbors told Robert that a few years back he had been interested in acquiring the property since it adjoined his own farm but the old lady had refused to even discuss selling it to him. The daughter had been in favor of selling it, but Mrs. Blake was fiercely adamant.

"She told me she was capable of tending to her own business and suggested that I should do the same. She said she had no intentions of selling her property to anybody. She said it was all she could leave her family, even if they didn't appreciate it, and that if anybody moved on to her place they would find themselves in a lot of trouble, more trouble than they could handle. Of course the daughter was embarrassed and so was I and rather than cause family friction, I withdrew my bid."

While the dozers tore at the land bushes, the contractor's work force razed the old house. The shingles were ripped from the roof, the rafters pried off and the walls pulled down. The lumber was oak, difficult to saw and nail and most of it went into the burning pile. Little by little, Mrs. Blake's home was fed to the flames.

The dozer operators had scheduled three weeks for the job but they didn't progress as rapidly as they would have had it not been for the swarms of locust that came from the field south of the house and settled on the machines and their operators. They swarmed in incredible numbers, forcing the dozer operators to take shelter in the barn and in their cars. They moved in when the dozers were starting up and left when the work was shut down. They eventually left, but not before causing added delays and costs.

It takes so few words to describe the culmination of so many months of planning and labor. Where once there were dirt tracks leading to a ramshackle old house surrounded by weeds, there was a modern ranch-style house at the crest of a tree-shaded lawn. There was an ample water supply. The barn had been remodeled and the land prepared for pasture and tillage. A deeply religious man, Robert often looked at his new home and gave thanks for his good fortune and family. Each member had contributed a share of labor and love.

The family was quickly accepted into the community. They moved their membership to a local church. Robert visited at the grain elevator and general store and Becky swapped recipes and patterns with the neighbors. They settled into a routine of peaceful rural life. And then it began.

One evening shortly after the family moved into their new home, Robert and his family arrived home from their weekly shopping trip. While Becky and the girls carried sacks of groceries and other purchases into the house, Robert went to the barn to check on the livestock. His chores completed, he started back to the house.

It was a few minutes past nightfall on a tranquil night. The insects' sounds had begun and there was a warm south breeze. The shadows lengthened under the maple tree as Robert stood and savored the evening's beauty.

As he walked to the house to join the others, he was startled by a plaintive cry, lasting perhaps fifteen seconds. He couldn't locate the source. It came again, louder. About fifteen seconds of shrill wailing, ending with a whimper.

He ran to the front of the house, thinking the cries might be coming from across the road. Beyond the road across from his house, the meadow was now moonlit, but the dark mass of trees at the far side of the field could shelter whatever was crying into the night.

The wailing came again, this time seeming to come from behind the house. Robert ran to the back of the house and tapped on the kitchen window, motioning to the girls and Becky to join him on the porch.

"Listen," he told them, "Something's crying, right over there." He pointed to a cluster of trees approximately five hundred yards southwest of the barn. The woods was silhouetted against the skyline in the early evening dark. The pasture between the trees and the barn lay half in dark, half flooded with moonlight.

There came the keening wail, building to a shrill cry and ending with a whimper.

"What is it, Daddy?" one of the girls whispered. "What kind of animal makes a sound like that?"

"It could be a dog," he said. "Maybe it's a wild cat, warning us off his hunting ground. They say there was a lot of them around at one time, but they've been gone for years. Maybe one of them came back."

The breeze had died down and the insect sounds ceased. The four of them stood on the porch at least a quarter hour, listening and wondering. The cries and whimpers continued in a pattern, fifteen seconds or so of wailing, a whimper, then silence.

"Whatever it is, I feel sorry for it," Becky said. "It sounds like it's badly hurt. But I don't think you should go see what it is. There's no telling what it might do."

The cries finally ceased and the other night sounds began. The family went inside for supper.

Robert made several trips to the back porch that night to stand and listen. The moon shone full and bright, the cattle moved around in the barn lot and the night creatures sang their songs. It was a pleasant evening.

The tenants who had lived in the house moved to a farm not far from Robert and Becky's new house, but the two families saw each other only occasionally.

One afternoon Becky was working on a set of drapes at the kitchen table. It was tedious work that she had been at since early morning. She was pleased when the telephone interrupted her work.

It was the tenant's wife calling. The two women talked of events that had happened since they last visited and chatted about community happenings.

"I've been wondering," the tenant's wife said. "Have you seen her yet?"

"Who?" Becky asked.

"You remember, I told you about the ghost. I didn't know if you believed me or not. Lot of folks make fun of such things."

"I remember you telling me about an old woman under the maple tree," Becky said, "but we haven't seen her yet." She thought of the cries in the woods.

"You will. I saw her several times. We saw her come out of that grove and walk across the pasture toward the house. We've seen her standing under that tree in the back yard, too."

"You mean someone else has seen her?"

"When my daughter was a child on that place, she saw and talked to her. Ask some of the neighbors who've lived around here for awhile. My daughter told some of them about talking to her..."

"Weren't you frightened?"

"Well, she never harmed anybody or anything. She'd just stand there. I won't say I wasn't uneasy, but she never threatened us or anything. Chances are you'll see her."

That night Becky told Robert about her conversation with the woman and her talk of the ghost.

"You know," he said, "they never did act unfriendly, but I always thought they resented being moved out. After all, no matter what it looked like, it was their home. She may be trying to frighten you."

"She doesn't seem like that kind of person at all. She's really very nice. You don't believe she and her daughter saw a ghost?"

"Of course I don't and you don't either. I've heard ghost stories, but no one had ever proved to me that they actually saw one."

"What about those awful sounds in the woods?" She said. "That's where the woman comes from, out of the woods."

"The sounds we heard don't have anything to do with her ghost story. There's a perfectly logical explanation for what we heard, if we only knew what it is. As for her daughter's chat with a ghost, children are always making up imaginary playmates. I'd put it out of my mind if I were you."

Chapter 4

A friendly, outgoing person, Robert enjoyed visiting with his neighbors, particularly Mr. Green, who lived two miles south of Robert's. Mr. Green's parents had owned Robert's property prior to Mrs. Blake.

Having lived in the area all his life, Mr. Green told Robert many interesting stories about the neighborhood. The most interesting stories were about Robert's farm.

"You know," Mr. Green said one time, "the old place didn't look like much when you bought it and there's been a lot of sadness there, too. Mrs. Blake's husband passed away while they lived there and she lost her father in a tragic accident. I think she had a daughter die there, too. Died real young. So the old house had its share of sorrows.

"We kept it up real nice when we lived there so it looked good when the Blakes bought it. We built the fence and that barn. My sister planted that maple tree in your back yard. She went out into the grove and dug it up roots and all and planted it herself. She said it would be here long after we are all gone, and I guess she was right.

"I used to feel sad when I'd pass and see how the place was so neglected. I'd remember the good times and how Mother and Dad and the rest of us took good care of it."

"Why did the Blakes led it go down hill?"

"It didn't look too bad as long as Mr. Blake was alive, but she didn't manage too well after he was gone. She held on, though. I guess the farm was all she had after he died and her daughter left home. She never asked anyone for help. Too proud, I suppose. Some of the neighborhood families offered to help at first, but she wasn't very friendly. She finally hired a tenant who lived on the property— the barn maybe. I've heard he could never do anything to her satisfaction. I guess she got a little twisted in her thinking during her last years, maybe from living alone for so long, but she was sure determined to hold on to what was her's." Mr. Green got quiet.

"Robert," he'd said, "I know you shouldn't say anything about another person if they're not around to defend themselves, but Mrs. Blake was sometimes downright mean. That's the only way to put it. She was damned mean."

"What did she do that was so mean?"

"Well, for one thing, she'd make friends with stray dogs that came to her place. You know, she'd feed them and talked to them.

Then, after she'd tamed them enough that they'd come when she called them, she'd put a rope around their neck and hang them in that maple tree in your back yard, the one my sister planted. I've seen them there myself, hanging and twisting. They'd howl and whine as the rope choked them. And that's not the worst part. While they were hanging there making those horrible noises, she'd jab them with a pitch fork, beginning with their eyes. It was horrible.

"She didn't just hang them in the maple, either. I have seen her drag them across the pasture with the rope, with their toenails digging into the ground, trying to get away. Then she'd string them up in a tree in the grove and start working them over with her pitch fork."

"Why didn't you turn her in?"

"Turn her into who? There wasn't any S.P.C.A. around here then, and you'd think twice before calling the law on a lonely old widow who probably reasoned that she was protecting her property. Everyone killed stray dogs then. If we didn't they'd form packs and kill our sheep. But she didn't have to kill them like that."

"Did you ever hear anything about a ghost that was suppose to show itself at the old house?"

"I guess everybody who's lived here very long has heard about it, but I never put stock in it myself. I did hear that the little girl that lived there claimed she talked to a ghost, but all I heard was second hand. I've never talked with anyone who actually saw anything."

A few years passed. The boys, Joseph and George, were born. They were good years. The cries in the woods and the tenant's wife's ghost story was all but forgotten.

When Joseph was four or five years old, he collected model cars, called match box cars or hot wheels. He accumulated an impressive collection of various sizes and models. He played with them for hours, rolling them across the kitchen floor and constructing runways and race tracks in the back yard sandbox. The cars were stored away at night on top the dresser in the boys' bedroom, carefully aligned. The cars and dresser top were off limits to the other children.

One night, the girls were in bed and Robert and Becky were watching television in the living room. George was already asleep and Becky told Joseph that it was time for him to go to bed. He went into the boys' room and Becky heard him arranging his cars.

Less than ten minutes later, Joseph called to Becky and said that someone was playing with his cars and would she come make them stop.

She went into the boys' room. The cars were in their usual positioned order. She told Joseph that he must have been dreaming about his cars, there was no one there and the cars would be there in the morning.

"Mother," he said, "I wasn't asleep. I wasn't even sleepy. I was just lying there with my eyes open and I heard the cars rolling. I set up in bed and looked at them and they were going round and round like crazy, real fast and close to the edge of the dresser. I couldn't see who was doing it but I wasn't asleep and the cars were rolling."

Becky went back into the living room, Joseph still protesting that he hadn't been asleep, that the cars rolled and she could have heard them herself if she'd listened.

Becky had hardly seated herself when Joseph cried out that his cars were rolling again, faster this time and he was afraid.

Robert and Becky went into the boys' room. The cars were still aligned, not moving. Joseph was crying, saying no one ever believed anything he said and that he'd sat up in bed again and watched the cars roll.

Becky sat on Joseph's bed, soothing and patting him. She told him she believed him and that she would sit with him and catch and punish whoever was bothering the cars. As she held her son's hands and watched the cars, she felt an uneasiness. The boy was so positive about what he'd seen.

Joseph finally went to sleep. Becky lay awake in her own bed until the early morning hours, listening to the sleep sounds of her family. Joseph cried out once and she ran across the hall and into his room. He was sleeping with his face toward the dresser. Becky sat and watched the cars awhile, again feeling a sense of uneasiness.

Chapter 5

At the time of the next incident, there were only two outside doors in the house. One exited from the kitchen to the back yard and was in constant use. The other was at the north end of the living room and was seldom used; it was to open into a family room, if and when they built one.

Both doors fit tightly, but winter wind and snow often drifted through almost imperceptible cracks at the bottom of the doors. In inclement weather, Becky folded towels and forced them against the door bottom, effectively barring wind and snow.

One winter night, there was a heavy, wind driven snow. The family sat up late watching television and listening to the storm. The ten o'clock weather report advised that travel was hazardous and all area schools would be closed the following day.

Robert rose early the next morning and looked in on his family in their warm bedrooms. The day was to be a vacation for them and he decided to let them sleep in.

He looked out the kitchen door toward the barn. The storm still raged and snow swirled around the corner of the barn, creating waist high drifts. The north side of the maple tree was plastered white and ice covered the small back porch.

Thankfully, the electricity had not been disrupted and he plugged in the coffee pot. The furnace was running in a constant roar. The temperature had plunged during the night.

He padded barefoot across the kitchen and into the living room. He felt a cold wind on his feet as he stepped into the living room and was surprised to see snow on the carpet. The oak inner door was opened against the living room wall, the towel bunched between the open door and the inner wall. Most of the carpet was cold and soggy. The snow must have been blowing in for some time.

He stared at the door, wondering who had opened it during the night and for what reason. It looked as though it had been unlocked, opened and the towel placed between it and the wall.

He locked the outer storm door and closed the inner door, leaving it locked, too.

He went back into the kitchen and put on his insulated coveralls and high top boots and stocking cap. He went out into the storm, angling his body against the strong, north wind and pelting snow. The drifts on the north side of the house were unmarked and there were no tracks on the driveway or lawn.

He tugged at the storm door and broke it loose from its iced edge. He attempted to open the door, an impossible task, for the towel wouldn't slide across the carpet. Coming back inside, rubbing and blowing on his hands, he stood once again and stared at the doors.

The family agreed at breakfast that there was a sleepwalker in their midst, but who was it?

Chapter 6

Robert eventually built his long-planned family room. The living room door that was mysteriously opened to the snow was now the entrance to the family room. A door at the west end of the new room opened into the garage, built at the same time as the family room.

A large wooden door at the west end of the new garage is manually opened, raised or lowered by means of a metal handle near the bottom of the door. Raising or lowering the garage door is a noisy happening. The door wheels scraping and clattering over metal tracks.

One night the everyone was in the family room. There was little conversation, each engrossed in homework or television. They were startled to hear the familiar screech of metal against metal.

Someone was entering the garage.

Robert opened the family-room door and switched on the garage lights. "Is someone there?" he called. There was no answer. Somewhat apprehensive, he walked around the car and opened the door. The dome light revealed there was no one inside the car.

He raised the garage door and went out to the driveway. There was no one there nor on the lawn. He walked around the house, calling out as he went.

"There's no one out there," he said when he came back inside. "I must have left the garage door raised when I came home and it somehow slid shut."

"Dad, you shut that." George said, "I was working in the barn and I saw you shut it before you went in the house."

"Well, whatever," Robert said, "I don't know where they went, but there's nobody there now."

Several times afterward, the family heard the garage door opening and closing, and they began to experience other sound and incidents. Sometimes a series of loud knocks on the family room door, storm doors opening and slamming shut. Lavatory faucets gushed water full force in the middle of the night. Quite often, the television changed channels by itself while they were watching it.

At first they were intrigued by the happenings, convinced that there was a logical explanation. Then they began to be concerned. A startling incident would take place, several days would pass, then another incident.

One night, long past midnight, the girls awakened to the sound of footsteps in the basement beneath their bedroom.

Someone was walking swiftly from one corner of the basement to the other. They listened as the footsteps hurried back and forth, then called their mother. When Becky came into the room, the footsteps ceased. To calm the girls, Robert went down into the basement. There was no one there.

Two weeks later the girls called to their parents that someone was walking in the basement again. The sound ceased when Robert and Becky came into the room, but as they listened there was a metallic clatter and a thud. Becky whispered that someone had run into her sewing table and knocked the yard stick and scissors to the floor. She knew the sound well. Immediately after, they heard the rattle of sewing supplies that she stored in a small metal cabinet that sat beside her sewing table. It sounded as if the cabinet was being shaken.

Robert confesses that he never felt less courageous in his life, but he and Becky went down the stairs together. The girls huddled together at the top of the stairs. Becky's sewing table and metal cabinet were undisturbed.

They checked in the basement storage room and under the stair way, finding nothing.

They slept little that night.

A week later. Becky woke to find the youngest daughter, Linda, standing by her parent's bed, trembling and in tears.

"I've been trying to wake you and Daddy," she whispered. "There's someone walking around in the living room. They're not even trying to keep quiet. They keep walking back and forth."

Robert had wakened and was listening to the footsteps. He

felt a chill of fear, but he slipped quietly from bed and went down the hall to the living room. The outside security light lit up the room and when Robert peered cautiously around the door, he could see the room had no one in it.

He checked the locks on each door and window, walked through the basement and the garage and looked in all the closets. There was no one in the house and no sign of entry.

Chapter 7

Robert and Becky discussed the happenings with their friends and relatives. All were interested. Some were obviously amused.

"You don't suppose the girls' imagination is working overtime, do you?" one asked.

"If it is, they're scaring themselves," Robert said. "I know that what Becky and I heard was not imagination. I also know there must be a logical explanation. There's been talk of peeping Toms in the neighborhood, but this all takes place inside the house. I don't see how anyone could get in and out so easily."

"Maybe it's spooks."

"I know it isn't anything like that, but it's beginning to get to us. The thing is, something startling will happen and we'll be upset for awhile. Then we'll kind of forget about it until something else happens. I'd sure like to know what's going on. Some people laugh about it, but it isn't funny to us. The kids are getting afraid to go to bed and Becky and I aren't getting much sleep either."

Robert and Becky were visiting neighbors the night Joan, the eldest daughter, saw the presence.

Robert had asked the children if they felt uneasy about staying by themselves an hour or two and had been assured that there was nothing to feel uneasy about. One of the girls told him that they weren't children anymore and were perfectly capable of taking care of themselves.

Robert thumbtacked a telephone number on the kitchen bulletin board. They were to call that number if anything unusual happened.

After the parents left, the girls washed the dishes and the boys did the outside chores. Afterwards the four of them watched television until the ten o'clock news came on, when the boys went to bed. After the news the girls retired to their room.

Linda began to breathe deeply in a few minutes and Joan lay on her back and thought about school. She curled on her left side, her favorite sleeping position. Looking toward the hall, she saw a light shining from the family room.

Linda was sleeping soundly, her arm across her face, and Joan could hear the boys snoring in their bedroom. She reluctantly left her bed and went down the hall to turn off the light.

As she reached the door leading into the family room, she stopped, terrified. In the northwest corner of the room, a corner unreached by the security light or the dim rays of the night light she'd gone to turn out, she saw the shadow of a tall, thin person distinctly outlined against the panel wall.

Leaving the light burning, she turned and ran down the hall to her room. She lay in bed, trembling and listening to the peaceful sleep sounds of Linda and the boys. She didn't know if she would be able to cry out if someone came from the shadows. She listened for footsteps. She couldn't force herself to go to the telephone in the kitchen. If she woke the others, they would all be frightened.

It seemed hours before lights flashed across the window as a car turned into the driveway. She heard her parents' voices as they unlocked the door. She met them in the kitchen, shaken and almost speechless.

Robert put his arm around her and the three of them went to the family room. There was no tall, thin shadow.

"Did you hear footsteps or a door shut after you saw it," Robert asked. "Was there noise in the garage?"

"There wasn't a sound. I don't know what I would have done if I'd heard someone walking around."

"Whatever you saw didn't move or come toward you? You didn't catch a glimpse of a hand or eyes?"

"No. It was just a dark shadow, Daddy, but it was real. It was the shadow of a tall, thin man or woman. I'm not going into that room by myself again."

Robert went through the house and basement, finding nothing. Becky promised to sit by Joan and stay awake until she went to sleep but it was in the early morning hours before Joan finally fell asleep.

Becky lay awake the rest of the night.

Robert and Becky became increasingly concerned over the effect of the incidents on their children. They were quiet and withdrawn, never indulging in their former boisterous mock arguments and roughhousing.

"We'll have to handle this carefully," Robert told Becky. "We can't make light of what the kids tell us. There really is something. I don't know what Joan saw, but she didn't see a tall man or woman standing in that corner. If we aren't careful, we'll all see shapes and shadows everywhere we look. Fright and imagination makes people see things that don't exist."

"Robert," Becky said, "you know it hasn't been all imagination. The children are actually frightened. They dread the nights and to tell the truth, so do I. Whoever is prowling around has no business here. They don't take anything, so they must be trying to frighten us, but why would anyone want to do that? I'm afraid to go in a room at night by myself and I keep listening for strange sounds."

"Well, I hate to admit it, but so do I. I feel so helpless. I don't know how to handle it or where to turn, but there must be some solution.

"There's a P.T.A. meeting tonight we should attend. Why don't you stay home with the kids? Heck, maybe I will, too."

"Robert, we can't stay home and never go anywhere. And we can't always go as a group. We'll have to work something out about going places until we find out who is causing all this grief.

You go tonight and I'll stay home with the kids. Just leave a telephone number where I can call you."

Before Robert left for the meeting he promised to come home after the business session and not stay for visiting and refreshments.

After supper, Becky, Linda and George sat in the living room while Joseph and Joan did their home work on the kitchen table. Darkness came and Becky turned on the lights. They were less frugal with the lights than they had been in the past. They left one light burning all night.

Becky could see Joseph from where she sat and she saw him look up from his papers and glance out the kitchen window. He looked back at his lesson, then out the kitchen window again. He left the table and stood by the window, his face pressed against the glass.

"What is it, Joseph?" she asked.

"We have company, Mother. A woman walked across the yard and stood under the maple tree. I thought she was coming in the back door."

Joan went to the window. "I see her," she said. "I caught a glimpse of her, but I don't see her now. She must have stepped back into the shadows."

Becky said it was probably someone with car trouble and went to the back porch. The security light lit up the yard and she could see no one near the tree. She called out that if there was someone there, they could come inside and use the phone. Her voice was strained as she called a second time and no answer. She thought of the tenant's wife's story of the woman under the tree and hoped the children didn't remember it.

She forced herself to go outside and around the corner of the house. There was no one on the lawn or in front of the house.

She ran back inside, locking the kitchen door behind her. She felt as if she were in a bad dream, running to escape an unseen presence. She told herself that she mustn't show fear, mustn't frighten the children.

She forgot about not showing fear when she was back in the kitchen. She yelled at Joseph, telling him he'd better not make up stories about seeing people in the yard, that they had enough problems without him adding to them.

Joseph shouted back at her. He said he did see a woman under the tree. He didn't know who she was and didn't care, but she was there. He said he was as frightened as Becky and asked why he would make up stories about seeing people in the yard, about spooky old women standing under the maple tree.

Becky put her arm around him. "Joseph," she said, "I'm sorry. It's just that I am so nervous and upset. I do believe you."

"Mother," Joan said, "I saw her, too. She was standing under the tree, then she was gone. Maybe she's in the barn."

Becky said she would turn on all the lights and call Robert. They hurried from room to room, turning on the lights and checking the closets. They went to the basement, leaving the lights burning when they came back upstairs.

"What good will all this do?" one of the girls asked. "Whatever it is can get in or out anytime it wants to."

Becky ran to the telephone and called Robert. At the meeting, Robert excused himself and hurried out the door. When he turned into the driveway, the house lights were on and he saw the family standing at the window. He left his car sitting in the driveway and ran to the kitchen. When he was inside, they all began talking at the same time.

"No one saw her but Joseph and Joan?" he asked.

Joseph was indignant and angry. "Why doesn't anyone believe me?" he said. "I did see her. She walked across the yard and stood under the tree. I hate this house. People go in and out any time they want to and we can't stop them. I can't even sleep nights anymore because I'm afraid there's someone in the house."

"Joseph, I do believe you," Robert said. "If you say you saw someone there, you saw her."

Robert went to the barn and walked through it, calling out as he went. He looked in the corn cribs and climbed up into the loft. There was no one there.

Chapter 8

One spring afternoon Mrs. Blake's daughter came to visit her home place. She was in her late seventies, hard of hearing and in poor health, but had a pleasant personality. She obviously enjoyed coming back to the farm, although her old home had been demolished.

She talked of her childhood and the hardships her mother endured to keep the farm after her husband died. She said she'd tried to persuade her mother to move to town to live with her, but she'd refused until her last years. She said her mother was "sort of set in her ways.

"She just stayed here and the old house fell down around her. I know the neighbors didn't appreciate the way it got to looking, but there wasn't anything I could do about it without her permission and she could be real stubborn. I hate to say this, but you've probably heard that her mind sort of wandered at the last.

"I worried about her a lot. She could have fallen and lain for several days without anyone knowing about it. No one ever visited her, although I'll admit that was a whole lot her own fault. I do wish people could have known her in her younger days. She always had big gardens and lots of flowers. Her flower garden was where your back yard is.

"She loved her blackberry patch, too. It was where your pasture is. She always said that her blackberry patch was the only crop that paid off on this farm."

Mrs. Blake talked about the fun she and her sister had had playing in the barn loft and under the maple tree. Robert thought of the tortured dogs hanging from that tree.

"She used to sew doll dresses for us and help us bake mud pies."

It was a different image of Mrs. Blake than Robert and Becky had heard.

"You people have sure improved the place. I'm not sure Mama would approve of the changes, but you have a beautiful home and I'm glad for you."

After the old lady left, Becky told Robert, "You know, we destroyed everything Mrs. Blake loved. We tore down her house and grassed over her flower bed and bulldozed her berry patch. I wouldn't blame her for being bitter, the way her life turned out. Suppose someone came along and destroyed everything we've built here?"

"It's not a fair comparison. If everyone was against improvement there'd never be progress. There will come a time when this will all be done away with. That's the way it's always been.

"Just the same, I have a different idea of the kind of person she was, at least to her family."

Mrs. Blake's daughter's visit seemed to trigger a series of incidents.

The boys were loud snorers. Almost nightly one of the girls would have to go to the boys' room and shake one of them or turn him over to stop the snoring.

Late one night the usual snoring began. Joan lay on her back, trying to will herself to sleep. Linda's rhythmic breathing was an added irritation.

Joan threw her covers off and went across the hall, half hoping she would wake someone else. She bent over George and laid her hand on his shoulder and the sounds ceased.

She raised up and glanced around the room as she waited to see if he would resume snoring. There was a shadow in the corner beside Joseph's bed, the shadow of a small, stooped person. In the shadow's right hand there was a long stick, evidently the handle to a tool, such as a rake.

It took all the courage she could summon to walk to the bedroom door. She looked back when she reached the hall and listened for footsteps or for movement in the shadows.

The next morning as she and Linda lay in bed, talking, she

told her sister what she'd seen.

"I know," Linda said, "I've seen it myself, usually in the corner by Joseph's bed."

"Why haven't you said anything about it?"

"I've never been sure of what I've seen. One minute it's standing there and the next it's gone. Besides, can you imagine what the boys will say if we say anything about it? I feel guilty not saying something about it, but I think we should be sure there's something there before we mention it."

It was not until several weeks later that the girls told the rest of the family about the shadow.

One afternoon Linda was alone in the house. She helped her mother clean the house and after Becky left for town, she settled down in the living room to read.

She read until she dozed off, but suddenly she sat erect. The timer on the kitchen stove was chiming. She'd not yet started supper.

As she listened to the timer, the kitchen door leading to the basement opened and shut. She went to the kitchen, shut off the timer and called down to the basement, "Is there someone there. Is that you, Mother?" There was no answer.

Becky arrived home a few minutes later. "We must have left the timer set and a breeze blew the basement door shut," she told Linda. It seemed a logical explanation and satisfied Linda until the next incident, two weeks later.

She had taken another day off. She had psyched herself into believing that a girl in her late teens could cope with harmless sounds.

However, when the family left, she was alert for unusual noises. She forced herself to go into the boys' room, half expecting to see a small stooped shadow. She was pleased with herself when she started the evening meal; she had stayed in the house all afternoon by herself.

She placed a pan of water on the stove and as she turned on the heat control, she felt a pounding against her foot. It thudded against her shoe sole three times. Someone was in the basement, hammering on the kitchen floor.

She stepped away from the stove and walked to the center of the room. She felt the pounding. It had followed her across the room.

At first she was terrified, then angry. The family had agreed long ago that they wouldn't play tricks on each other. She remembered that she'd been home all afternoon and hadn't seen anyone come home. She tried to call down into the basement but her throat was tight and she couldn't form words.

She went back into the living room and sat where she could see the basement door. She considered stopping a passing car, but wondered what the neighbors would think of grown girl frightened by sounds from a basement.

At last Becky's car turned into the drive and Linda met her at the door, almost incoherent.

"Well," Becky said, "if you've been watching the door, whoever was there is still there. We'll go see."

"Mother," Linda said. "you know you won't find anything. We never do. But I'm not making it up; I did feel the pounding against my feet."

Linda was wrong. Becky did find something. An old unkempt mop always hung on the storage room outer wall. It hadn't been used for days.

The mop was lying on the basement floor, directly under the kitchen table.

One morning Linda told Becky that she and Joan heard sounds in their bedroom at night.

"What kind of sounds? Are they knocks or foot steps?"

"No. A different kind of sound. The first time I heard it I thought Joan had gotten out of bed and was opening and closing her jewelry box, like she was choosing something to wear. I thought it was such a silly thing to do so late at night. Then I got scared when I couldn't see anyone at the dresser. I looked at Joan's bed and she was lying there sound asleep. I woke her up and she heard the sounds too. We were both scared, but the sounds finally stopped."

"Has this happened more than once?"

"Several times. And that's not all. Sometimes the perfume and cologne bottles rattle and shake. When that happens, an odor stays in our room until morning. It's a wonder you and Daddy can't smell it."

"What does it smell like?"

"A strong, sweet smell, like dead flowers. Like someone sprinkled perfume all over the room."

"Is the jewelry out of place or is there perfume missing?"

"Not that we can tell. But it does happen. You do believe me, don't you?"

"Of course I believe you. You know how concerned your

father and I are over what's happening. Haven't you been frightened?"

"I'll say we have. I don't know which is worse, to hear the sounds and not see anything or to think that some night we will see something. Mother, what do you think is causing all these things to happen to us?"

I don't know, but I do know we are going to find out. I want you to call me the next time anything happens. There's no reason to keep it to yourself. We can't find the cause if we can't hear it.

The girls never heard any more sounds at the dresser after Linda talked to her mother.

Chapter 9

The bizarre incidents continued. Sometimes a few days would pass without incident, then several would take place within a matter of hours. One time, they heard loud pounding noises in the basement. There were knocks at the doors and windows. The lavatory faucet was turned on in the middle of the night.

One morning after a sleepless night, Becky told Robert that they must have another talk about the problems in their house. "It's not going to go away and it's beginning to affect us all."

"I know that. Do you have any idea what we can do?"

"Yes, I do, but you're not going to like it. You remember the articles we read about supernatural happenings in other peoples' houses? I think there is something to them. Some have even moved from their homes and the things that frightened them are the same things that have happened to us."

"You mean you actually believe all those stories? That's the kind of thinking that sells magazines."

"I don't know what I believe or think, but do you have any other explanation for what's happening to us?"

Robert shook his head. "I don't have an explanation so far, but that doesn't mean that there's not an explanation. I do know that if we start talking about ghosts and haunted houses, we're going to frighten the kids worse than they are."

"I don't agree. They're not children any more and they've grown up knowing there's something wrong here. I think we should discuss every possibility with them, no matter how far fetched it seems. We won't gain anything by refusing to talk about it."

The six of them sat up until late that night talking about their experiences and about how the cases they had read so closely resembled their own. The children were not as disturbed as Robert had thought they would be.

"Suppose such things do happen—and I'm not saying that they do," Robert said, "how do you handle anything like ghosts?"

Becky looked up. "I've read that certain people were trained to help families with such problems."

"I've read those articles too," Robert said, "Do you want strangers in our home with their mumbo jumbo and their seances? I wouldn't want my customers to know we were dealing with ghost busters. We'd be laughed right out of church."

"We don't have to broadcast it, but we can at least talk to somebody who knows about such things. What's wrong with talking to our minister?"

"Before we talk about haunted houses and spirits, let's visit with someone who claims it's happened to them. We'll find out that no one has any real proof."

The family began a study of supernatural experiences and supposedly documented case histories. Many of the accounts were similar to their own, some were more frightening. There were tales of poltergeists and appearances and unexplainable incidents. They read Biblical accounts of demons and witches and possession. Robert visited neighbors to learn whether any of them had heard stories about Mrs. Blake's home and was surprised at how many of his neighbors had their own family legends of sounds and appearances. He was also surprised that the stories were taken quite seriously.

One elderly neighbor told him that there had been a group of people some years ago who held seances in their homes. "They'd meet at each other's houses and hold weird ceremonies. They were said to be devil worshippers, but you know how talk like that gets around. There was probably nothing to it. I always wanted to go to one of their meetings, but my folks wouldn't let me. You don't think about something like that going on in this community, do you? But there was a good sized group of them at one time."

"Do you know if Mrs. Blake was a member?"

"I don't know about that, but she was an odd one, alright. I guess just about everybody around here has a story about that old place of hers, but it's like most tales; it always happened to someone else."

"Becky," Robert said, "you wouldn't believe how many of our neighbors have stories about things that happened in their houses. Most of them were sounds that couldn't be located, like our knocks. Some of them heard footsteps in rooms that were supposed to be empty. And you know, they sounded like they believed every word of it."

Becky visited briefly with their minister's wife one Sunday morning and began to tell her about their problems, but they were interrupted before she could finish. The minister's wife suggested that they get together soon with their husbands and hear the entire account.

The house remained quiet for several weeks.

Chapter 10

Mack, their dog, had come to the family as a pup. He out-grew his big-footed, clumsy stage into a handsome, gray and white adult, big shouldered and thick bodied. He was a Norwegian Elk Hound, gentle with the children and compatible with adults. He assumed the responsibility of guarding the house and barn and took those duties seriously. He was not surly or hostile toward visitors, but he made it clearly understood that he was on watch over his family's property. He was dearly loved.

He loved them all in return, but he was partial to Becky. After the rest of the family left for the day, Becky usually allowed Mack to come inside and he would go to the basement with her and sleep near her feet while she sewed.

One morning she was working at her sewing table and

Mack was lying near her with his body limply folded and his head on his paws, his favorite sleeping position. He lay relaxed, his legs occasionally twitching as he dreamed.

Becky stopped sewing when she saw the big dog suddenly stand erect. He hadn't stretched and yawned as he normally would have coming out of a deep sleep. His body was tense, his head cocked to one side, his ears erect.

"What is it, Mack?" she said. "Is there someone here?" His tail wagged. He heard her, but he was still on guard. He looked toward the basement stairs, stared at Becky and looked back toward the stairs again. He was telling her to listen.

She waited, expecting a knock at the door. Mack was still on his feet. He wasn't barking, his usual way of announcing visitors. He shifted his gaze to the basement storage room, then walked stiff legged over to the little room and stood at the door. He snarled and his teeth were bared, his face close to the storage room door.

"What is it?" Becky said. "Is there something in there, Mack?" He gave no indication he heard her.

Becky opened the storage room door and Mack went inside. He sniffed in the corners and behind the air conditioning unit. His tail wagged and he licked Becky's hand when she patted his head and rubbed behind his ears. He went back to his resting place and quickly fell asleep when Becky sat back down at her sewing table.

She worked quickly as the moments passed. Mack slept soundly although once she thought she heard him growl or whine.

Shortly after, she heard growling sounds again, harsh rasping noises as though the dog was having difficulty breathing. The rasping sounds ended in a whimper.

The snarling, rasping sounds came again and again, each ending in a high pitched whimper. Becky waited for Mack to waken. Whatever he was doing, he was doing it in his sleep. Becky shouted at Mack to wake up. The big dog lifted his head and opened his eyes. His tail wagged vigorously. The noises ceased.

Becky finished her sewing and Mack continued his nap. There were no more sounds, but Becky watched Mack closely as he slept.

When Mack was six years old, he became increasingly clumsy. Once he missed the top step and fell off the back porch. He no longer hunted in the meadow and in the grove. He stopped going to the basement with Becky. He was as affectionate as ever, perhaps more so, but he whined and complained often. He was showing all signs of senility.

One morning, Robert went to where Mack was lying under the maple tree. The big dog stood to be petted, but Robert struck an open handed slap at Mack's face, stopping just short of actual contact. Mack never flinched. His eyes were clear. Mack was blind.

Robert and Becky took Mack to a local veterinarian, but he was unable to diagnose the problem. He said Mack was in superb physical condition and his eyes appeared normal, but he was totally blind. The vet suggested they take Mack to the University Small Animal Clinic where there was more sophisticated diagnostic equipment.

The University veterinarian told Robert and Becky that

Mack's problem was the most baffling case they had handled and asked permission to perform exploratory surgery. The operation, they said, was routine and posed little danger, but it would be impossible to form a medical opinion without it.

Mack came through the surgery in great shape, but the doctors still couldn't find the reason for his loss of sight. The University refused payment for the surgery, saying nothing had been resolved. They said Mack would eventually learn to compensate for his blindness, but he might never see again.

Chapter 11

The basement storage room is barely large enough to contain the air conditioning unit and half a dozen cardboard boxes filled with cast off toys and other outgrown and forgotten articles.

A ledge about four feet high and three feet wide was left along the south side of the basement when it was excavated and Robert concreted it for use as a storage shelf for canned fruit and vegetables. A part of it is the south wall of the storage room. The east end of the shelf in the storage room is stacked with books and magazines, most of them Robert's text books and agricultural publications.

The basement is a large, comfortable room and was Becky's sewing work room for several years.

One warm afternoon, she was doing her laundry as she

sewed. The upstairs windows and doors were open and she could hear the pleasant afternoon sounds. Sunlight shone downstairs through the open kitchen door. She had switched on the basement overhead lights for better sewing light. There had been no unexplained incidents in the house for quite a while.

She sewed as the washing machine whirled and spun to a stop, readying the clothes for the dryer. Remembering some problems she'd had with the dryer door falling open, she decided to hang the wash outside and began piling it into a plastic clothes basket. She worked swiftly. It had been a busy afternoon and there was still a pile of unfinished work on the sewing table.

As she removed the last few articles of clothing from the washer, she was startled by a loud noise inside the storage room, followed by the sound of shattering glass. In a moment of panic, she thought the south basement wall had collapsed. She snatched up her clothes basket and ran up the basement stairs to the top landing. As she reached the landing, she remembered that the sound had come from inside the storage room. She looked back downstairs; the basement wall was intact. She realized what had happened and was embarrassed by her mad dash up the basement stairs. Somehow, a fruit jar had fallen from the concrete ledge and on to the storage room floor.

She went back down to the storage room and looked inside. A broken jar lay on the floor and pieces of glass were scattered throughout the room; some had even flown up on the top of the air conditioning unit. A thick, hardback book was lying on top of a pile of shards in front of the air-conditioning unit.

The longer she stared, the more frightened she became. The jar lid was lying at least five feet from the ledge. The books and magazines were stacked at the east end of the ledge, past the canned fruits and vegetables. It looked as though the jar had been thrown to the floor and the book lifted over the jars and onto the pile of glass.

Becky slammed shut the storage room door and ran back upstairs. She leaned against the kitchen table, unable to control her trembling. She thought she heard the storage room door open and the sound of footsteps in the basement. She knew the sounds were imagined, but she couldn't bring herself to go to the stair and look down into the basement. She buried her face in her hands and began to cry. In a few minutes, she picked up her basket of clothes and ran outside.

She considered stopping a passing car or calling a neighbor. What would she tell them, that a jar had fallen from a shelf and frightened her? After she hung the wash, she pulled weeds in the garden. She walked around in the yard and barn yard, then pulled weeds again.

She knew she couldn't go back into the house alone. She wondered what she would do if the boys came home early, hungry as usual. She prayed that Robert would arrive first.

She was standing in front of the barn when Robert and Linda came home. Robert waved and smiled until he saw her clasped hands and drawn expression. He stopped the truck and ran to her.

"What is it?" he asked. "Has something happened to one of the kids?"

"Robert," she said, "there's something in that basement and

I don't know what it is." She was trembling again and he put his arms around her as she told him what had happened.

In the basement, the lights were burning and the storage room door was closed. Robert eased the door open and started to step inside the little room, but stopped when he saw the piles of glass on the floor. The floor would have to be swept before he walked on it. He recognized the book as one of his favorite texts about livestock rations. He thought he had stored it under a pile of magazines at the east end of the shelf.

Neither of them commented on the happening as they swept the floor. Then they sat in the kitchen and talked.

"Becky," Robert said, "it had to be a rat or some other kind of animal. That's all it could be."

"We've never seen mice in the house, let alone rats. We would surely have heard them. And how could a rat throw a jar and a book five feet?"

"I don't know, but it's my guess that a rat bumped a jar off the ledge and the book was lying on top the jar instead of with the other books."

"I'm almost as afraid of rats as I am of some of the other things that have happened. I don't want to tell anyone that we have rats in our house. We can get rid of them, can't we?"

"Of course we can. I have something at the store that I'll guarantee will get rid of them."

Rats do possess great strength in relation to their size and it was possible that one had pushed the jar and book off the ledge. Becky was embarrassed by her hysterical flight from the basement and asked the family to not mention it to anyone. They didn't, but there was some teasing over her "super rats." They were all convinced that the presence of rats in the house explained many of the sounds they had heard.

After the rest of the family left the following day, Becky stood on the bottom stair step, looking at the storage room door. She half expected it to slowly open, or worse, open suddenly or violently. She forced herself to move forward and open the door, stepping inside the dark, little room. Though shivering with fright, she methodically re-stacked the books and magazines and rearranged the fruit and vegetable jars.

She went out into the basement and opened and shut the dryer door a few times, welcoming the familiar clang, then sat down at her sewing table. At first she sat straight and tense, her hands clasped on her lap. After awhile, she relaxed. There were no other sounds in the basement. The dryer door remained shut. The whirrrrr of the sewing machine punctured the silence.

What she had done was not an act of defiance. It was something she had to do or she knew she would never work in the basement again. She worked at her sewing table most of the day without interruption.

That afternoon, Robert brought home a ten-pound bag of rat poison. The directions read to place the small, green pellets behind boxes and other objects the rats could run behind. Rats live a fearful, furtive existence and prefer to not travel in open spaces. The label cautioned not expect immediate results as it would take several days for the rats to die. The pellets should be fed consistently and for an extended period of time. Becky shuddered when she read that the sight of one rat indicated that there were possibly dozens of the creatures in the area.

That night Robert poured several piles of the poison on top of the concrete ledge. He heaped more poison behind the air conditioning unit and behind boxes and jars. It was a costly banquet. He used over half a bag of the pellets.

The next morning, Becky heard him moving boxes and jars in the basement. He was smiling when he came back upstairs. "It was just as I thought," he said, "it was rats. They ate every pile of bait I put out; never left a crumb. We must be invaded with them. Strange, though, the bait is gone, but I didn't find any other rat signs. I couldn't even find where they get in and out."

That evening, Robert brought a rat trap home. The trap was a wire mesh, funnel-shaped construction, designed with a series of doors opening inward so that when the rat enters the trap to get to the bait, the doors lock behind it. Robert placed the baited trap behind some of the magazines.

The next morning, Becky went to the basement and sifted flour around the trap and over the ledge and magazines. A rat would leave footprints in the flour if it came to the trap.

Robert checked the trap that evening. The bait was gone and there were no prints in the flour.

"Robert," Becky said on the morning the bait disappeared and the flour was unmarked, "you and I both know we don't have rats in our basement. You said yourself that it would have taken hundreds of them to eat all the poison you put out, and we've never even seen a sign of a rat. There is something in that basement and it's not rats. I'm scared."

Robert nodded. "I know." From that time on, there was no further talk about rats.

Not long after, Robert stood in the doorway to the kitchen and announced. "I'm ready to talk to someone if you are. Only, I don't know who to talk to. I never in my life thought I'd look for someone to talk to about our house being haunted. I just don't want everyone to know about it."

"We don't have to tell your folks or anyone else if you don't want to, but let's find someone who can help us. We can't go on this way."

"I don't blame you and the kids for being scared. To tell the truth, I am too, some of the time. There's something here and it's not rats and it's not imagination."

Chapter 12

The Sunday after they decided to seek help, Robert and Becky visited Becky's sister Rose, who lived in the St. Louis, Missouri area. Rose was fascinated as Becky told her of their experiences and how their fear had grown until they knew they needed help.

Becky said, "We've tried to put up a good front, but we just can't live with it any more; we never know what's going to happen next. We never seriously thought of spirits before, but we don't know what else could cause it. People wouldn't believe what we've been through and I know it is hard to believe, but it happened just the way I told it."

Rose was touched by her sister's distress and they held hands and talked as they had in times past. Rose told Becky that she knew her and Robert too well to think they would invent the story. She said, "I wish you'd told me sooner. It's always good to talk to someone, especially a sister. Have you thought of talking to a priest or a psychic? I would have looked for help long ago."

Becky told Rose that they didn't know who to contact. "None of our friends have had experience with psychics and as for ghosts, you should hear some of the comments we've heard about that."

Wednesday night, after the Sunday visit, Rose called Becky. "I didn't tell you Sunday," she said, "but one of our neighbors is a well-known psychic. She has worked with the St. Louis police on several occasions and she's been interviewed many times.

"I wanted to talk to her before I called you so I called her Monday night. I told her my sister was convinced there was a presence in her house and I'd like to talk with her about it sometime.

"She called an hour ago and said she'd had a dream last night. It was such a vivid dream that she got out of bed and wrote it down. She dreamed she saw an older woman talking to a younger one. She didn't recall the entire conversation, but she remembered the younger woman telling the other one that she should go back where she came from.

"But that's not the strangest part. I asked her what the women looked like and she described them and, Becky, the younger one was you. As far a I know, she's never seen you and I tried to remember if I'd ever shown her a photo. I know I haven't, but she described you perfectly, just as if she'd known you all her life. There's no doubt about it; you were one of the women in her dream."

"Did she tell you what the older woman looked like?"

"Yes. She said the older woman was small and wore her hair in a bun. You know, the way older women used to tie up their hair. And she was standing bent over at the waist."

"Do you suppose your friend would come to our house and let us tell her what's happened to us?"

"I'm sure she'll come. I'd probably have a hard time keeping her away."

Becky told Robert about the psychic's dream. "Are you thinking what I'm thinking?" she asked.

"That the older woman in the dream was Mrs. Blake? We can settle that. The neighbor who bid on the farm before I did knew her as well as anyone. We'll ask him what she looked like." Robert drove to his neighbor's house that evening.

"Yes, of course I remember what she looked like. She was a small woman, sort of bent over like a lot of older folks. Arthritis, maybe. I don't know."

"Do you remember how she wore her hair?"

"She usually wore it tied up on her head in a kind of a knot. Another thing, she almost always carried a cane or a pitchfork she used for a cane."

Becky called Rose after Robert came home with the information. "Your friend gave a good description of Mrs. Blake. Only, our neighbor said Mrs. Blake usually carried a cane or a pitchfork."

"Oh, my God," Rose said. "Becky, I hung up before I finished telling you all the dream. My friend said one of the strange things about the dream was that the older woman was holding a pitchfork."

Becky shivered, "Will you call her tonight and ask her when she can come and see us?"

Chapter 13

Rose and the psychic arrived at Robert and Becky's house the following Wednesday. The psychic smiled and told Becky, "I don't feel as if I were meeting a stranger. Rose told you about my dream?"

Joan had stayed home from work and the four women visited awhile. The psychic asked if it would be alright to tape their conversation. Becky said that she didn't mind taping or anything else that would help the psychic understand their problems.

"Becky, I'd like you and Joan to tell me everything you remember about your experiences. I'll hold consultations with my colleagues and they'll listen to the tapes, too. No detail is unimportant. I'll need to know what took place, the date, and time of day and how many witnesses there were. Take your time; I have all day. Tell me everything."

Becky and Joan began at the very beginning and on to the latest incident. When they paused from emotion or an attempt to remember a detail, the psychic gently questioned them. Was the family in a group during this particular incident? Had Mrs. Blake been described to them before they saw the shadow in the boys' room? Had they ever felt physically threatened and were objects thrown about?

They taped until noon, then sat down to lunch, but the psychic stood by the kitchen window for a few minutes. Her body was rigid and her hands clenched. She sat at the table and asked it the word blackberry had significance. Becky said that they were told that Mrs. Blake was very fond of her blackberry patches and might have resented its being bulldozed.

The psychic said she'd felt a presence near her and it had whispered something about blackberries.

After lunch, the psychic suggested they record incidents as they happened in the rooms where they took place. Becky said they should start in the basement, where many of them were experienced.

In the basement, the psychic asked them to step inside the storage room, to show her how far the book and jar had been thrown, but she remained outside. She remarked that she felt cold and a little sick to her stomach.

As they talked, Mack began barking furiously out by the maple tree and there was a loud pounding on the top stair landing, lasting several minutes before the pounding ceased and Mack stopped barking.

"I have all this on tape," the psychic told them. "Incidentally,

I am as frightened as you are. I know we don't want to cross that landing, but let's go upstairs and finish taping."

When they reached the kitchen, they saw Mack sound asleep under the maple tree.

"I'm sorry I didn't go in the storage room," the psychic said, "but I felt quite ill and I had a strong feeling that I shouldn't go inside that room."

She told Becky that she would like to take photographs inside and outside the house. She said images that were invisible to the human eye sometimes were captured on film.

She snapped photos of each room and the basement, then went outside and took pictures of the house, and barn and the maple tree. She told them that when she photographed the window of the boys' room, she saw a presence in the window, the image of a small person, bent at the waist and with its hair done in a bun.

Later, as she and a colleague studied the photos, they saw a second image beside the figure she had seen. It seemed to be the image of a small child, a little girl.

When Becky learned of the second image, she called Mrs. Blake's daughter and asked if she had another sister beside the one they knew.

"Oh, yes, I had another sister, but she died when she was just ten years old. I don't think anyone knew what she died from; she just sort of wasted away. Mama never got over losing her that way. There wasn't anything she could have done, but she always thought she was somehow responsible for my sister's death. She was never the same after that."

After the photo session, the four women sat at the kitchen table and talked.

"I know how difficult it is for you to accept the fact that there is a presence in your home," the psychic said. "You have tried to explain all that's happened as natural reasoning, but it's not natural. You'd be surprised how many families have had similar experiences.

"It's my opinion that you do have a presence in your home. A very strong presence. I think it is the lady who used to live here. Certainly the shadow the girls saw and the older lady in my dream fits her description. Naturally you are frightened, but I don't think she is an evil spirit at all. I don't think she will harm you, but she doesn't want you here and she is telling you she doesn't. Frankly, I was frightened in the basement, but it was only because I felt the presence so strongly. In fact, I felt it from the moment I walked into this house.

"You said that living under this stress, never knowing what will happen next, is getting to be more than you can cope with. That's what she wants—and she's winning. I realize you will be more nervous now that you know who it is, but I must be honest. My advise is to have this house blessed and ask her to leave. She is trying to impose her will on you and you must not let her win."

"What do we do?" Becky asked.

"Call the local priest, tell him what you told me and ask him to bless this house. This probably is not the first time he's been called for that purpose. I can assure you he will be discreet. Frankly, I don't think you'll ever rest easy in this house until it's blessed.

"I have this entire day on tape, your account, the sound we heard, everything. I'll study the tapes and photos with the people I work with, but I can tell you their advice will be the same as mine. Have this house blessed and the sooner the better. I say again that I don't believe you are in any danger, but the presence must be made to leave."

After Rose and the psychic left, Becky called Robert and told him of the day's experiences and the psychic's advice to have their house blessed. As they talked, the books on the shelves in the family room began sliding back and forth and slamming into the wall. Joan was crying and as Becky talked with Robert, the pots and pans in the kitchen began clanging against each other.

Robert and Linda hurried home and Becky retold her story of the day's happenings. "Robert," she said, "there's no doubt in my mind now. She's here and she wants us *out*. She may be listening to us right now. We have to have help."

"Becky, I promise you I'll take care of this right now. We'll either get help tonight or we'll all spend the night at a motel. I'm going to call Dad and tell him what's going on and what we're going to do."

He dialed his father's number but when John answered there was such buzzing, humming sounds on the line that conversation was impossible.

"Son, what is going on," John asked.

"I'll call you later," Robert shouted into the phone.

"Call the priest," he told Becky.

The priest, whom they did not know personally, was courteous and sympathetic. "You must understand," he told Becky, "That it's not merely a question of wanting to help you and your family and the fact that you are not members of the Church has nothing to do with it. I must have permission from my superiors before I can act. We study the facts and determine whether there is definite evidence of possession and if you are in physical danger. It will take a little time to document the evidence and from what you told me, you are in no mood to wait while we deliberate and I certainly don't blame you. What I can do now is to counsel and pray with you. Since counsel and prayer is all I can offer at this time, would you consider calling your pastor?"

Becky replied that although their minister was a devout, compassionate man and a close, personal friend, she felt that he was not persuaded that there are supernatural happenings and psychic phenomena. She said she had discussed their problems very briefly with their pastor's wife.

"I'm sure you are correct about your minister's opinion of supernatural happenings, but this is not a case of believing or not believing in something. Your pastor has a family in his pastorate in need of his presence and his prayers. If you still want to visit with me after you call your pastor, I'll be glad to: tonight if you wish. First, call him. I think you'll find him eager to help as a friend and a minister, regardless of his opinion as to the source of your problems."

Chapter 14

Their minister was in his study when they called. He was accustomed to being summoned at all hours. He might have suspected marital problems with some couples, but that was unlikely with Robert and Becky. He could gather little from Becky's excited call except that they needed him as soon as possible. He recalled that Becky had mentioned some sort of problem to his wife, but he didn't remember the details.

He told his wife there was a family that needed counsel and that he might be late, a common occurrence in his household. He felt most useful to his congregation at those times. He had always contended that any qualified speaker could deliver inspirational sermons and any serious scholar could interpret scripture, but true religion best proved its practical application in times of need. He marked his Bible where he had been reading, folded his notes into his reference book and went to his car.

As he opened the car door, he felt a strange, strong sense of reluctance. He didn't want to go to the family's residence. It was a feeling he'd never experienced. Perhaps, he thought, it would be wiser for them to work out their own he thought, it would be wiser for them to work out their own difficulties. Why should he be judge and advisor? He turned to go back to his office and call Robert that he wouldn't be able to visit with him that evening.

But he recalled Becky's obvious distress. The family was dear to him. How could he tell them to solve their own problems? He dismissed the strange feeling of reluctance from his mind and drove to their home.

Robert came out on the back porch to greet him. He had always been captivated by Robert's ready smile and buoyant manner, but tonight Robert seemed tense and troubled.

"What is it," the minister asked, "Has there been a death in the family?"

Robert shook his head and motioned the minister inside. Robert and Becky sat at the kitchen table with the pastor and the children leaned against the cabinet and living-room door. An experienced counselor, the minister knew the family was needing the answer to a problem, a problem he could not even guess. He smiled at them and told Robert, "talk to me."

"Pastor," Robert said, "we should have called you long ago. Years ago. We were not sure what your attitude would be toward what is happening to us and what we think is causing our problems.

For approximately an hour he told the minister about their experiences. Occasionally, Becky or one of the children would remind him of an incident. The house was quiet except for their conversation. Robert concluded by telling of that day's events and the psychic's suggestion that their house should be blessed. He said he knew their denomination did not admit to possession and manifestations, but they had turned to the pastor for prayer and comfort.

He said, "You must believe me. All of us have seen and heard things we can't explain and we are convinced there is something in this house that we can't control. We didn't believe it at first either, but we can't explain it any other way. We're not imagining all this. It must be made to leave or we're going to leave. I can't ask my family to stay in this house and I don't want to either. It would be hard to walk away from everything we've built here, but we can't live like this anymore."

The minister knew he was expected to say something and he prayed mentally as he searched for words.

"Folks," he said, "I have no idea what's causing your problems. I only know what you told me and I know you and your faith. And I know you need me. Frankly, I never felt more inadequate in my life. First we will go to the one who knows all and is willing to help us with our problems even when we don't know what the problem is. I don't know any ceremony or form for what we will do, but He will hear us whatever we do. We will join hands and pray that you be released from your fear. I am convinced that your real problem is fear of something you can't explain. Essentially, I will bless this house in His name. We will bless each room at a time."

Robert suggested that since many of the happenings took place in the basement that they bless it first. The children were reluctant to go near the storage room so Robert opened the storage room door, the minister began to chill and his stomach churned. He was nauseated to the point that he told them he would be unable to pray at this time. The three of them went back upstairs.

"Folks," the minister said, "we can't let fear keep us from talking to God. All of us are going to go into that storage room and pray."

They stood in a crowded circle in the little room and the seven of them joined hands. The preacher felt the perspiration on Becky's hand and she was trembling. His stomach was still churning and he was shaking with cold. He wondered if he could finish his prayer before he emptied his stomach. He told the family to speak up if any of them felt or saw anything.

He prayed. He didn't know what he was praying that the family be delivered from or what he would say or do if there actually was a manifestation. He blessed the family and the house and asked that the family be freed from the fear that possessed them. He consecrated their lives and his own to future service and he prayed that everlasting peace might rest on the house. He noticed that Becky had stopped trembling.

They went back upstairs and he repeated his prayer in each room. The house was quiet except for his prayers. Afterward, they sat in the living room and talked. It was past midnight. The preacher had prayed for almost two hours.

Glancing at his watch, he said, "Now, I want all of you to

understand something. I will not give serious thought to ghosts or spirits or anything like that. There are no such things, in this house or anywhere else. Your house is not haunted by an older lady who has come back from the dead to frighten you. But, I do believe in good and evil and I sincerely feel that what we have here tonight was fear, just fear. That's what you have felt all along. I have no doubt that you have had experiences you can't explain. I didn't just imagine what I felt in the basement, either, but I know it wasn't a ghost that caused it. Just remember that there is nothing so evil that prayer and faith cannot overcome it.

"I think I'll call my wife and tell her I'm staying the night with you, if it won't inconvenience you. I can sleep anywhere. The family room will be fine."

"Pastor," Robert said, "I feel more at ease than I have in months. We all do. You'll never know what your prayers mean to us. I'm sorry we didn't call you sooner. I would much rather you go home to get some rest. We are all exhausted from this day and night and we need sleep, too. I really feel that there'll be no more problems tonight, but if there are we'll come stay with you."

When the minister left, Robert and his family were preparing for bed.

Chapter 15

The minister recorded his impression of the house blessing approximately a year later. The tape is a discussion with the family, but the minister's recollections are as follows:

"You called me early in the evening but I wasn't home at the time and I came down about nine thirty, right?

"We spent at least forty-five minutes just discussing the situation. I told you when I got there that I was skeptical. I remained skeptical the entire evening.

"Now, I have a wild imagination. It's always been wild, ever since I was young. I had some idea of what the call was about. My wife had mentioned it to me, but I didn't know any of the details. But I could have sworn I felt jittery about going down there. I still think it was my imagination or nerves more than anything else.

"But after about forty five minutes of stories about the occurrences, I was convinced that something really was affecting the family. You were obviously frightened. Fear was the problem, more than anything else.

"We went through the house and blessed it room by room. The procedure was to ask God to remove the fear. I couldn't convince myself that there was a ghost in the house.

"We went to the basement first. Again, it could have been my imagination, but in the basement I was cold. There was a spot right in front of the storage room that was cold. You'd back up to where the sewing table is and it wasn't cold, but in front of that room it was freezing. And inside the room, it was worse.

"We assembled there and said our first prayer. There was a time that I became nauseated and I thought I might not finish. I thought I was going to throw up right there in front of everybody. But we did finish and the nausea left.

"We went through the house room by room, but that was my only feeling out of the ordinary during the entire evening. I did feel greatly relieved after we finished praying in the basement and the nausea left, but the rest of the house was fine. I got a little bored around midnight because it just kept going on and on. I began to wish it was just a three-room house.

"I stayed there until twelve thirty and would have willingly stayed the evening because I had become quite interested. But I did know something was affecting the entire family and I sensed a feeling of relief when the blessing was over.

"One of the exercises we went through was that each member of the family would proceed from the living room and into the basement and into all the rooms of the house, alone. Linda could not have done that before the blessing and Joseph would have refused. So at least we accomplished that much.

"The strangest thing, though, happened to me at the end of the evening; something that still bothers and effects me. That evening I realized for the first time how powerful are the forces in this world that we don't understand and we can't control.

"At twelve thirty, I started home and I had a feeling that I wasn't alone as I drove. As I said before, I have a strong imagination. You know, I see the curtains in the heat vent and I imagine someone is trying to come in through the window; things like that.

"But there was something with me. I kept telling myself that it was my imagination, but when I got about a mile from your house, I looked in the rear view mirror and there were two of the brightest red eyes I have ever seen, looking back at me. I stopped the car and turned and looked, but there was nothing there.

"I got out of the car and looked on both sides of the road and there was nothing that could have caused a reflection; no house lights, no reflectors, nothing.

"From that point on, I drove home exceedingly fast. I wanted to get out of the dark and into my home and be with someone I could talk to. When I got home, I shared my experience with my wife and we went to bed, but I had such an uneasy feeling that I couldn't sleep.

"Now, this was in May. Around the first of June, I began to have feelings of anxiety when I was in the dark or when I was alone. When I was driving alone, I knew I wasn't really alone because I felt a presence. Sometimes it felt as though there was a hand on my shoulder and it sent chills through my entire body. The feeling would come and go, but I was convinced it was just something in my mind.

Then, one night I was working late in my office and I felt the presence. When I was writing or typing or whatever, I'd have a chill when the presence touched my shoulder. It would spread through my entire body and if I tried to ignore it, it would go to my head. And my head would actually become numb.

"It wouldn't be there all the time and I got to where I'd know when it was going to happen and I actually began to talk to it. I thought I was losing my mind.

"I had to share it with someone and I went to a friend, a fellow minister, and talked with him about it. We called it a spirit removal, but it was actually an exorcism. He suggested that I try prayer.

"I guess the whole time something was happening that I intellectually didn't consider. I thought it was all in my mind and that I could conquer it, but I couldn't. My friend said that if prayer didn't work, perhaps I should have a session with psychiatrists.

"I came home that night after talking with him and told my wife that I would spend the night in the office and conquer it.

"There were times before that. I know I'm skipping around and I apologize, but I'm taping it as it comes to me. One other evening I was working late. This is when it all came to a head. The presence came into my office while I was working and I yelled at it and told it to go away, but it wouldn't leave. I became very frightened and felt the fear that must have gripped the family all along, for no reason at all. That's what scared me the most. There was no rational reason for me to be frightened.

"I was so frightened that I ran out of my office without turning off the lights. I ran into our bedroom and woke my wife. She got up and went to the bathroom and I couldn't stand being alone. It was as if I were three or four again and locked in a dark closet and my mother wasn't there.

"Before she got back to bed, I guess I dozed off or something because I imagined a woman coming into the house. I don't know how she got in, but she stood at the door and pointed a finger at me and said that there was someone near me that wanted to kill me. At that point my wife came back to bed and I woke up and I couldn't be alone that night.

"That week I visited my friend again and shared what had happened with him. I was quite concerned that I was losing my mind. When I tried prayer, it worked, the presence would leave. Or if I read scripture, it would leave. But as soon as I stopped praying, it would come back. Some nights this would go on all night. And it still happens that way, although not as often. Prayer still works, but it always comes back.

"The experiences the family had leads me to believe that what we are dealing with has nothing to do with spirits or ghosts or goblins or anything like that, but with the devil, Satan. There is no scriptural teaching that supports the presence of ghosts or witches or anything like that, but there is a great number of references pointing to the power of Satan and demons that possess animals and places and people. I strongly believe that that is the realm we are talking about. It can never be totally gotten rid of.

Chapter 16

"There was a period of relief after the house was blessed. For awhile, there was no startling occurrences, no unusual sights or sounds.

"However, within five or six weeks after the blessing, Robert and Joseph went through a frightening period of their lives. They find it difficult, today, to discuss their emotions and actions during those trying times.

"Robert had never been seriously ill in his life. He was proud of his good health and physical condition and thought it was a personal weakness to miss work from "feeling bad." Pessimism and negative thinking was not a part of his normal personality.

"Shortly after the house blessing, he became deeply depressed. Business was good, the farm prospered and the house was quiet, but he became morose and withdrawn. He spent hours at the office by himself. He avoided contact with friends and relatives, preferring to stay home and worry, not knowing what he was worrying about. He was so rude to some of his customers that they took their business elsewhere. He was aware of being surly and rude, but seemed unable to control himself.

"He describes his feeling during those times as being like two persons in one body. He had read of out of body experiences, but says he never felt that he left his body. Rather, it was as though he were two separate personalities.

"The family never knew what mood to expect from him. At times he was tyrannical, expecting instant obedience to his whims. Other times, he was permissive and indulgent. He suffered spells of melancholia with brief returns to his former buoyant personality.

"Some days he awoke to a throbbing headache which usually persisted until mid-morning or noon. He suffered from chronic back ache and often stayed home to lie, miserably, in bed.

"He collapsed at home one morning and was off work a month. One physician said he showed symptoms of stress and told him deep anxiety could lead to severe head and back pain. Daily, painful back therapy was prescribed.

"Equally disturbing was the animosity that developed between Robert and Joseph. They had always enjoyed a close relationship and had formerly spent long hours together planning livestock and farm projects. Now, they argued almost constantly, usually over trivial matters. Becky could hear them shouting at each other while doing the chores and family meals were seldom serene.

The rest of the family was embarrassed by their bitter arguments over minor differences. Nothing the boy did pleased his father and Joseph became sullen and uncooperative.

"There was a dramatic change in Joseph's personality and attitude. He had always been cheerful and outgoing like his father, but he became arrogant and quarrelsome with his mother and abusive to his sisters. The family's good-natured bantering with one another changed to frequent angry confrontations.

"Joseph began walking in his sleep. Robert and Becky would hear him wandering around in the house in the early morning hours, sound asleep when they went to him. He shuffled in aimless circles, talking to himself. Several times they found him standing by the kitchen window, looking toward the barn and mumbling meaningless phrases. Sometimes he went into Linda and Joan's bedroom and yanked violently at the closet doors.

"If Becky spoke to him during his sleep walking, he was infuriated, shouting at her to take her hands off him and leave him alone. At those times, his voice was deep and guttural, unnatural sounding.

"In spite of their day-time differences, Joseph would allow only his father to lead him back to his room.

"He resented references to his sleep walking, insisting that he slept soundly every night. He said he didn't know why everybody lied about him. He did admit to his parents that he often dreamed of doing "bad things," but they were only dreams.

"One morning he told them about a particularly vivid dream he'd had the previous evening. He dreamed of floating through the house to the basement door. He started down the basement stairs, but a cold, vaporous cloud rose up the stairs toward him and he was terrified. He thought if he could only call his father, he would be safe, but he was unable to make a sound. He said he woke in his bed trembling and perspiring.

"He said he'd had other dreams of going down to the basement and it always seemed important that he go inside the storage room, but he was always too frightened to open the door.

"Robert and Becky thought it best not to tell Joseph that they had followed him through the house to the basement door the previous evening and saw him open the door and stand on the top landing. There was a terrified expression on his face and he trembled violently as he tried to form words that came out as gibberish. Robert laid his hand on his son's trembling shoulders, spoke gently to him and lead him back to his bedroom."

Chapter 17

One of Robert's garden-supply customers was a pleasant, obviously well educated, middle-aged lady. She and Robert often discussed soils, and fertilizers and weed control. She was better informed than most of his customers.

One morning, Robert mentioned his physical problems and his daily therapy and told how he had been informed that stress may contribute to such problems.

She remarked that one's mind has greater effect on physical condition than many people realize. "Medication can only do so much." she said, "then we must learn to help ourselves by using our minds."

Seeing Robert's quizzical expression, she said, "I don't know your feeling about spirituality and mind, but I am psychic. My mind works with the mind of one who consults with me and I have been able to help relieve stress and even locate objects and people."

Robert told her briefly of some of the experiences he and his family had had and about how they consulted with a psychic from St. Louis.

She was extremely interested in his account and offered to visit his home if they felt they needed further opinion as to the source of their problems.

She paid for her purchases and started to leave. She stopped at the door and turned to face Robert again. There was an intent, questioning look on her face.

"Who is Joel?" she asked.

"Joel? I don't know anyone named Joel. Why do you ask?"

"Can you remember a Joel, perhaps someone you knew in the past? Try very hard to think of someone named Joel who was a part of your life in some way."

"I am thinking, but I'm sure I've never known anyone named Joel. It's such an unusual name I believe I would remember it."

"Don't be frightened, but I have a strong impression that someone named Joel is trying to reach me through you. There is a presence with you and its name is Joel.

"I think, if I were you, I'd try to find out if there ever was someone named Joel who was connected with your life in some way. You may have forgotten, or you may be mentally blocking it out, but I have never received a stronger impression than I am receiving right now. You have my phone number. You may want to call me when you find out who Joel is."

That evening the family discussed Robert's experience with the psychic. They were interested in her appearance, if she seemed to be in a trance or spoke in unnatural tones. They were disappointed to learn that, like the psychic from St. Louis, she was not unusual in appearance or actions and seemed mainly interested in potting soils and fertilizers.

Days passed. The house remained quiet and Robert's health improved, if only slightly.

One morning at breakfast, Becky said, "Robert, do you suppose there was a land owner or tenant connected with this farm before the Greens or the Blakes? I know we aren't having the problems we had before the blessing, but suppose there was a Joel. Wouldn't it be easy to make him go away? I know you don't like to talk about it and I know you are better, you and Joseph, but you are still not yourself. You don't eat well, and you don't sleep well. You may not know it, but I wake up at night when you get up and stand staring out the window. Things are going so much better now and you need to think about yourself."

"Becky," he said, "I don't believe in possession any more than you do, but I still have these strange feelings, like two persons in one body. And the oddest thing is that I don't know if it would be right to make it go away. I don't want to scare you, but maybe we should talk about it. If there is a Joel and he is trying to live again, I'm not sure it would be right to ask him to leave our house. I know it's crazy, but I keep thinking about what we went through before. If we send him away, and I'm not saying there really is a Joel, will we be sending him to hell? Maybe he is trying to stay away from some place and that's why he has come back. I don't know what to think. This is the most ridiculous conversation we've ever had, but if there really was someone living through me, I have this feeling that we should leave him alone and not make him go away."

"Let's call the minister. It worked before and it'll work again, Robert."

"There's another thing I've thought about. If we send this one away, will the other one come back? I believe the pastor when he says there are no ghosts and spirits, just good and evil, but maybe we'd be letting the evil back in."

"Whatever's causing you to feel like you do, I don't know how you could avoid calling it evil."

"I'll tell you something I can do. I'm going to the courthouse and search the papers on this farm. Maybe I'll find Joel in there somewhere."

Robert went to the courthouse the next morning and a clerk helped him search the records. They didn't have to search for very long. Mrs. Blake's father had signed some of the papers.

Mrs. Blake's father was named Joel.

Chapter 18

After discovering who Joel had been, Robert visited with a neighbor who had lived in the area many years and asked him if he had known Mrs. Blake's father.

"I knew him very well. He visited his daughter quite often. He was a nice old man; I never heard anybody say anything against him. He died a hard death, though."

"What did he die of?"

"He was murdered. If I remember right, he'd sold some livestock and swung by this way to see his daughter. He was riding horseback and carrying his money with him. I don't know how much money he had, but he was way laid on the road and robbed. He must have put up a fight. I don't know about that either, but he was shot and killed. Shot in the head."

"Did they ever find out who did it?"

Oh yes. They caught the fellow who did it and he was hanged. The trial and hanging were the biggest events of the year. Joel was a well-liked man. Mrs. Blake, poor old soul, had more than her share of grief."

"Oh, Robert," Becky said when she heard of Joel's tragic death, "it's no wonder she lost her mind. She went through enough to make her lose it. Her husband and little girl died here and her father was murdered while she lived here. I'm more convinced than ever that we did the right thing by having the house blessed. I believe she left, but now there must be another one. I still think we should talk to the minister again."

"I don't want to ask for help until we need it. Look how long it's been since anything's happened."

"I know we haven't seen or heard anything, but you still aren't yourself. You still have your moods and bad days and I know you worry over possession even if you deny it. Would you rather talk with the pastor or have Rose and the psychic visit us?"

Robert shook his head. "Let's wait and see. So far nothing's happened for awhile. Maybe it will stay that way."

One morning, a week after Robert discussed Joel with the neighbor who had known him, Robert and Joseph were working in the barn.

"Dad, something is going on in mine and George's bedroom. It's happened several times, but I didn't want to talk about it and scare everybody again."

"What is it, son? Are you having nightmares again? You haven't been sleepwalking for a long time."

"No. It's not like the other things that happened. I know it sounds silly, but I've been wakened several times by someone squeezing my toes. The feeling is strong enough that it wakes me up each time. I always sit up in bed and wonder if I should call you, but I lie back down and usually drift off to sleep again."

"Have you told George?"

"No. Like I said, I haven't told anyone until now. We have all been more relaxed since the house blessing. I thought our troubles were over. I don't dream it, though. The pressure's too strong for it to be a dream."

"I want you to call me the next time it happens. I want to know when these things take place. We don't have to go through what we did before."

The following morning, Joan asked her father if there had been company at the house the previous evening. Robert said there had been no visitors and that he and Becky had gone to bed shortly after the girls.

"Then I had a strange dream. There was a man in the house, an old man. When I saw him, it seemed too real to be a dream."

"What did he look like?"

"He was a tall, thin older man with long, white hair. He was wearing a funny-looking old fashioned coat and a floppy black hat."

"Weren't you frightened?"

"No; that's the funny part. I felt as if I were awake and

dreaming at the same time and he seemed like such a nice man. He didn't touch me or anything. He just stood beside the bed and looked down at me. Then he smiled and turned to leave the room. When he reached the door, he looked back and smiled again. Then he went down the hall to the kitchen. I knew it was a dream, but I didn't seem to be asleep. I could see everything in the room and Linda asleep in her bed, but I wasn't scared because I knew I was dreaming. He must have stood there a minute or two; I had plenty of time to see him. Daddy, do you suppose I was dreaming about Mrs. Blake's father?"

"I don't know. I don't know what her father looked like."

When Robert and Linda arrived at the store that morning, he called the psychic who had sensed Joel's presence. It was only a matter of minutes before she drove into the parking area.

"I've been expecting to hear from you," she said. "And I need insect powder."

Robert smiled. "My family was disappointed that you were not more mysterious acting."

"You mean spooky acting, don't you? I'm just a housewife with a special gift. I'm as bewildered as anyone by the things I see. Long ago, I felt like a freak, but not any more. Even when I was young, I knew certain things were going to happen before they took place. Sometimes I was frightened by the things I sensed. Now I know I have a divine gift. Since it was a gift, I've never charged a dime for a consultation. Whether or not others believe in the gift doesn't bother me at all. It's each individual's choice to believe or disbelieve. By the way, have you discovered who Joel is and why he chose you?"

Traffic passed, the town went about its business and customers came and went as Robert told her the entire story of his house, ending with the house blessing and Joan's dream. Linda came to the office door and interrupted him.

"When you sensed a presence with Daddy, did you have an impression of what it looked like?" she asked the psychic.

"Not a clear picture, but I did receive an impression that it was an older man. Perhaps it was the man in your sister's dream." The psychic turned her attention to Robert. "What connection did Joel have with your family?"

Robert told her about searching the records and discovering that Joel had been Mrs. Blake's father.

"Do you still feel as though you are two persons in one body?"

"Yes, but I can live with that. I just want my family to be free from worrying all the time."

"Robert, this is very important. Don't you really feel that you don't want to get rid of the other presence?"

"That's it exactly," he said. "It doesn't seem right to make it go away. It's not hurting me or anyone else."

She was silent a moment. "I don't want to frighten you," she said, "but that is indicative of true possession. You feel you would be destroying a part of yourself.

"You are not the first to experience that feeling. Almost every family has legends of supernatural events. Many people think that admitting such things do happen that they are contradicting their religious faith. The most familiar stories are about a knock or series of knocks, or the smell of flowers or footsteps in an empty room.

"You did the right thing by having your house blessed, but I'm convinced the blessing was only partially effective.I still think that Joel is trying to live again through you. You are partly convinced yourself or you wouldn't have called me. Hardly anyone likes to think of himself as possessed, especially someone as pragmatic as you.

"Joel is not necessarily an evil presence, just a lost one. From his appearance and actions, he is quite the opposite of evil. You have been feeling and acting as you have because you are fighting something you don't understand and something you never believed could happen to you, or to anyone else for that matter. How many of your friends understand possession? Neither did you. For your peace of mind, Joel must be made to leave."

"How do we do that?"

"We don't. This is something you must do by yourself. Ask you pastor to come pray with you again, but first ask Joel to leave. Go somewhere around the house, not necessarily in it, and tell Joel he is frightening your family and he must leave. Tell him to not be frightened and to keep going toward the light."

"The light?"

"He'll understand. He'll know what you mean."

"Robert," Becky said as he discussed his conversation with the psychic, "we've talked this over so many times. I say let's call the minister right now."

"First," he said, "no matter how foolish it sounds, I'm going to ask Joel to leave."

Robert went out to the barnyard. There was a large fallen tree south of the barn, and making sure no one was in the barn to hear him, he seated himself on its trunk.

"Joel," he said aloud, "I don't know if you are listening, but if you are trying to live through me, you know how confused I am. We know you are a nice person and won't hurt us, but we are frightened. That's why we asked our minister to bless our house. You are trying to live where you don't belong. Your daughter and your friends are not here anymore. Don't be afraid. Just keep going toward the light and you'll be going where you belong. We know you're not bad, but it's bad to frighten us this way. Please, leave us alone and go where you belong."

A breeze rustled the leaves. A tractor hummed in the distance and a car passed along the road in front of the house. Robert wondered what the people in the car would think if they knew he was talking to a man who had been dead many years. He sat silently, half expecting to feel a light touch or hear a whisper. Nothing happened. He walked slowly to the house.

The family sat in the living room that evening and Robert related his talk with Joel. They each felt a sense of apprehension, but they made small talk and managed a laugh at Robert sitting on a tree trunk, talking to a dead man. Robert said he felt they might have to ask for help again; but they knew who to call this time. If any of them saw or heard anything, they were to let Robert know. There was no reason for one person to carry a burden of fear alone.

As Robert talked, suddenly disturbing sounds came from the kitchen, like the dinner glasses being slammed against the kitchen cabinets. They expected to hear glass shattering. When Robert ran into the kitchen, the pounding ceased.

"Everybody stay calm," he cautioned, "I'm going to call the pastor."

The minister had just arrived home when Robert called. "Pastor," he said, "will you come down and spend a little time with us?"

"Are you still having problems in your house?"

"Not as bad as they were, but there are some things we want to talk about."

"I've had some extraordinary feelings myself that I'll discuss with you some day. Of course I'll come. Tonight?"

"Yes. Please do. We need you."

When the pastor arrived at the farm, they told him of the psychic's belief that Robert was possessed by Mrs. Blake's father, Joel. They told him about the older man in Joan's dream and they were almost in tears as they related Robert and Joseph's personality changes and their bitter arguments. They told him how Joseph had shuffled through the house at night muttering gibberish and how he yelled at his mother and sisters in a strange-sounding voice.

The Minister decided not to reprove them for their obsession with spirits and possession. They were too upset for any attempt at rationalization.

He said, "Now, it is your belief that there is a presence in this house, perhaps more than one, and that this presence can hear what we're saying at this moment?" They nodded in agreement.

"If this presence is listening, it should be able to move that tray if we ask it to, am I right?"

Linda said she knew it could do it if it were asked and it wanted to.

"Alright. I'm asking it to prove its presence," the Minister said. The tray remained motionless.

"Of course it could be said that the presence just didn't want to move the tray," the Preacher said with a smile. "I'm not minimizing your fear.

"Essentially, what we will do is to perform an exorcism," he said. "Now, I'm sure there are certain proscribed exorcism rites, but I know nothing whatever about them. I do know that the Son of God is able and willing to overcome all evil, even evil that may exist only in our minds. We will ask Him to help us again.

"This is what we will do. I will read certain passages of Scripture and we will join hands and pray, just as we did when we blessed the house. I want each of you to concentrate on a truth. That truth is that Jesus, Himself, is here with us, right now. You have told me that you believe there is a presence that may be listening to us even as we speak. You must tell yourself that He is here with us also, because He is. Never let go that thought.

"If any of you have a sensation or feel a presence, you are to let me know immediately, even if it's in the middle of prayer."

"That's odd," he said, "I seem to have forgotten my Bible. May I use your's?" Linda brought him one of their family Bibles and he opened it at random. He glanced at the pages and seemed surprised.

"I can't believe this," he said, "it opened to the specific section I had wanted to read." The passages were from the Book of Mark, the ninth chapter:

"One of the men in the crowd spoke up and said 'Master, I brought my son for you to heal. He can't talk because he is possessed by a demon and whenever the demon is in control of him, it dashes him to the ground and makes him foam at the mouth and grind his teeth and become rigid. So I begged your disciples to cast out the demon, but they couldn't do it.'"

"Jesus said to his disciples, 'Oh, what tiny faith you have. How much longer must I be with you until you believe? How much longer must I be patient with you? Bring the boy to me.'

"So they brought the boy to him, but when he saw Jesus, the demon convulsed the boy terribly and he fell to the ground writhing and foaming at the mouth.

"'How long has he been this way?' Jesus asked the father. And he replied, 'Since he was very small, and the demon often makes him fall into the fire or water. Oh, have mercy on us and do something, if you can.'

"'If I can?' Jesus replied. 'Anything is possible if you have faith.'

"The father instantly replied, 'I do have faith. Oh, help me to have more.'

"When Jesus saw the crowd was growing, he rebuked the demon.

"'Oh, demon of deafness and dumbness," he said, 'I command you to come out of this child and enter him no more.'

"Then the demon screamed terribly and convulsed the child no more and left him and the boy lay limp and motionless, to all appearances dead.

"A murmur ran through the crowd, 'He is dead.' But Jesus took the boy by the hand and helped him to his feet and he stood up and was alright.

"Afterward, when Jesus was alone in the house with His disciples, they asked Him, 'Why couldn't we cast the demon out?'

"Jesus replied, 'Cases like this require prayer.'"

As the minister read the passages, the others thought of Robert's weeks of depression and Joseph's terrifying nightmares and they felt a closeness to the grieving father and his son. The compassionate words spoken two thousand years ago moved them deeply.

After the Scripture reading, they all joined hands as they sat at the kitchen table and the minister prayed. It was a prayer confessing weaknesses and doubts and a plea for understanding. The minister told Jesus they knew He was with them and was willing to help them. The family was unaware the minister was praying for himself as well as them. He hadn't yet told them of his personal problems after the house blessing.

As the minister prayed, Joseph suddenly cried out, "Help me. I'm spinning around in the dark. Please help me." The others opened their eyes and looked at Joseph. His eyes were closed and his body was rigid, his hands clenched at his sides, but he was not moving.

The pastor cried out in a loud voice, "In Jesus' name, leave this house and that boy. Begone! In His name."

Joseph sobbed, "It's no use. I'm still spinning."

The pastor rose to his feet and shouted, "In Jesus' name, leave. Leave the boy alone."

There was a brief silence and then Joseph spoke in a strained but calm voice, "I'm alright. I'm not spinning any more. I'm alright."

The pastor continued praying, a prayer of thanksgiving. The house was quiet. There was only the sound of the pastor's emotional prayer. When he finished praying, much later, there was a feeling of peace within each of them.

After prayer, the minister said, "Let me tell you all this. I do not believe, and will never believe, that there are spirits in your house, but I have no doubt that we have been in the presence of something evil. I wouldn't leave now if I didn't believe that whatever was here was conquered. We all have this feeling of relief, but call me again if you need me. Tonight, if you wish. I can be here in a matter of minutes."

Chapter 19

The minister recorded his recollection of the exorcism as follows:

"Well, it's a difficult thing to describe. I told what I felt the night of the blessing on the other tape, and that was that I felt cold and nauseated.

"The second time, I didn't have that feeling. This time, I felt that we were doing something useful and that we had help.

"But what was accomplished both times could have been done by the family. It was accomplished by the strength of God, not through the strength or skills of any individual. Anyone could have done it. All we had to do was to realized that we had something to fight and that we couldn't fight it by ourselves and we have to ask God for help. It's the same thing as when I had those other feelings after the blessing and I still have them. I have to keep telling myself that I cannot fight it by myself. I have to ask God for help. That's what's important. Now, I felt His presence there. I wasn't able to see it, but I didn't have to. It's interesting. That first night after the blessing as I went home, I felt a presence in the car. The night of the exorcism, I didn't feel that presence because I felt God's presence.

"After Robert called that night, I went down to the house and they all described their sensations and fears and told me about Robert's melancholia and moods. And, about Joseph's experiences.

"All this just strengthened my feelings that what we were dealing with all along was Satan himself. And we conquered. The family was being told that there was the good spirit, its name was Joel and there was Mrs. Blake, the bad spirit. But even if there had been two, they were both extensions of the same thing. If we don't stop talking about good spirits and bad spirits, we'll lay ourselves open to being hurt again. If they were here, they were merely extensions of the same thing—evil.

"I don't know why I didn't bring my Bible that night. I believe it was Linda brought me their family Bible. It was strange, but when I opened that Bible, just at random, it fell open to the passages that fit our case. I couldn't have had a better selection if I'd looked for it. I think it opened to Mark's account of Jesus' curing the demonic boy. It's been awhile and I've forgotten the exact passages. Mark's gospel is filled with references to demons and possessions of humans and animals and Jesus' conquering them. We asked Him to conquer this one and He did.

"I hope you bring out in your manuscript that this was not a bunch of—you know—it's not a sensationalist thing. It's not a story about goblins and ghosts and things like that. It was about the presence of evil in this world and about evil attacking a family, trying to shake the foundation of their faith and how their faith triumphed. And it was nothing else.

"Psychics may have come in this house and talked about spirits and possession and things like that—there probably are people who can sense the devil's presence. But I'm more and more convinced that if we don't stop calling it good spirits, and bad spirits, and cute little witches and things like that, we are leaving ourselves open to evil again. And it would be even more difficult to just let God take over.

"When you dwell on spirits, and good witches, and goblins and such things, you're saying that somehow you, with your sensitivity, can change things—but you can't. No matter how man tries to fight Satan, he's going to lose unless he calls on God. And that's the truth." End of Tape

Chapter 20

The family and I communicated regularly during the months of structuring the volume of notes into sequence and readable form. The tapes contain almost two decades of remembrances and were corrected or clarified each time we visited. The family was determined that there would be no sensationalist aspect to their account. They wanted to tell their story exactly as it happened. It was a time-consuming chore to record it, but a fascinating one.

A year and a half after Robert and I visited at the family reunion and I learned of the presence in their house, the rough draft of their story was finished. All that remained was a final proof reading by the family and myself and I could begin the final typing.

I called Becky one morning to inform her that the manuscript was in its ending stage and to thank her for her patience during the long period of transcribing and writing.

"Steve," she said, "you haven't talked to Robert?"

"No. Should I have called?"

"It isn't finished. They're back with us."

"You mean a presence is back? Which one?"

"We don't know which one, but we know at least one is back."

"I thought the exorcism was the end of it."

"It was, as far as the house is concerned. Now it's in the barn."

"You have the same problems in the barn that you had in the house?"

"It's not the same, Steve. It's scarier this time. In all the years in the house, we never felt that we were in real physical danger. That's not true this time. There have been a couple times that at least one of us could have been badly hurt."

The following week, I drove down to talk to the family.

It began in the barn as it had in the house, with incidents that were puzzling, but not frightening.

The barn lights are operated by pull cords attached to the fixtures. There are wall plates along each side of the barn for extension cords. The boys always listen to the radio when they work in the barn. They are especially fond of loud rock music. The last person to leave the barn at night is responsible for turning off the lights and the radio.

One evening a few weeks after the exorcism, George was alone in the barn, finishing his share of the chores. When they were completed, he walked through the barn, turning off lights and unplugging the radio. The barn was pitch dark as he walked outside and toward the house.

As he reached the maple tree, he heard rock music blaring and turned to see the barn ablaze with light. Perplexed, positive he had tended to the lights and radio, he went back inside the barn and turned them off again. The barn stayed dark and quiet. He went into the house, washed his hands and joined the others at dinner.

The following week, Joseph told his father he thought there could be problems with the barn wiring. He said that several times he had been sure he had turned off the lights, but they would turn back on after he had left the barn. He asked if it was possible there was a short in the wiring and reminded Robert that there was a lot of straw piled just above the wires.

The next day, Robert pulled the wires from the meter box and traced them back to the fixtures and wall plates. The wiring was in good shape and there was no malfunction of the fixtures. The puzzling happening occurred every week or so during that summer.

Robert is understandably proud of his brood cow herd. It is the culmination of years of selection and breeding. A profitable herd requires livestock know how, dedicated labor and a large capital investment. A herd's state of health is of constant concern. It is an economical loss and an emotional experience to lose a cow or a calf. Robert has watched most of his herd grow from wobbly-legged, bawling calves to huge, docile "milk factories" as he calls them.

He and the boys were quite concerned when, over a short period of time, many of the cows became extremely nervous and excitable. They occasionally ran from one side of the pasture to another for no apparent reason. One prized cow was found lying dead in the grove west of the house. She had been dead several hours, too long for an autopsy to determine the cause of her death.

"I don't understand it," he told the boys. "She hasn't even been off feed. She was alright the last time I saw her. Do any of the others seem sick to you?"

"They don't act right," Joseph said. "They spook easily and they don't want to go into the barn, even at feeding time. When they do go in, sometimes they run back out again. They seem to be afraid of something in the barn. I wouldn't want to be in their way if the whole herd decided to run out at the same time."

Joseph's fear of a stampede came true a few days later. To get the cows to go in to the barn, they were treated to a palatable ration called Range Blox, large nutritious pellets with a high molasses content. The herd loved the Blox and usually came running to the barn when the boys poured it into the wooden troughs inside the barn. To avoid being surrounded by the big animals as they rushed to the feeders, Joseph barricaded the barn door with wooden gates which he removed when the troughs were filled.

One afternoon the boys barricaded the door and poured the Blox into the troughs. The herd milled around, bawling, and pushed into the barnyard, shoving against the wooden gates. Joseph removed the gates and he and George stood to one side to let the cattle run to their favorite ration.

Joseph suddenly shouted, "Watch out, George" and they both ran across the barn away from the door. The herd had stopped eating their favorite food and were stampeding toward the barn door. They were bawling and their eyes rolled as they thudded against each other in a panic. If the boys had not moved quickly, one or both of them could have been crushed against the wall or gone under the cows' hooves. It was almost an hour before the cows began moving slowly back into the barn, one at a time.

The hog pen inside the barn is separated from the cattle feeding area by a wooden plank fence. Several times a week, the hogs stopped eating, too, and ran outside the door, squealing and shoving one another. Sometimes, they stayed out of the barn several hours, returning slowly and cautiously.

"Dad," Joseph said one morning, "there's something in that barn that's spooking the livestock. I don't know what kind of varmint it is or how it gets in, but we'd better trap it. The hogs aren't putting on much weight and, to tell the truth, the way they are acting, I don't like to work with them.

When a brood cow is within a few days of calving, she is caged in a pen in the barn where she can be watched and cared for in case of calving difficulty. Many night trips are made to the barn during calving time, to check on the cows in the maternity pen.

One night the boys drove one of the cows into the barn and to the maternity pen. She appeared ready to calve at any time.

Joseph woke early the next morning and hurried to the barn to check on the mother. The miracle of birth never loses its fascination to a farm boy and a healthy calf means added farm income.

He heard the calf bawling as he neared the barn, but when he looked into the maternity pen, the calf was backed into a corner, bawling loudly and its mother lay dead in the other corner.

The veterinarian performed an autopsy and told Robert he was unable to determine the cause of death. "Robert," he said, "have you lost any more cows as suddenly as this one?"

Robert said he had lost several head. None of them had appeared to be ill and each had died suddenly.

"I'm really not sure what happened to this one," the vet said. "The vital organs are in good shape, the heart and liver show no signs of deterioration and the lungs are normal. I have no idea why she died."

After the veterinarian left, Linda told her father that she had heard pounding in the barn the previous night, but had assumed that Robert was repairing a stall. It was not unusual to do night repair work during calving time.

"I was out there at two o'clock this morning," Robert said, "But I didn't do any repairing. What time did you hear the pounding?"

"I don't know. I never did get wide awake. I may have heard you open the screen door and it slammed shut."

"It was more likely one of the cows kicking the side of a stall," he offered, half-heartedly.

Chapter 21

George was working with newly-born calves one Saturday afternoon. He went from stall to stall, pitching fresh straw on the pen floors and adjusting water buckets.

As he bent over one of the buckets, wiring it to the pen, he was surprised to see straw and dust sifting down through the cracks in the loft floor. Something was moving across the straw-covered loft floor above him. He shrugged. The cats often hunted mice in the loft. He turned back to his work.

Pieces of straw continued to fall and he thought, for a moment, that he heard footsteps. He went over and turned off the radio. Heavy footsteps walked across the loft, from the west wall to the east.

"Is that you, Joseph?" he called. No one answered. He ran

out of the barn and across the yard to the house. Robert and Becky were in the kitchen.

"Dad," he said, "there's someone in the barn loft." He told them about the straw and the footsteps. "I don't know who it is and I didn't try to find out," he told them.

Robert went out to the barn, telling George to stay with Becky. He called out when he stepped inside. Hearing no answer, he climbed to the loft. It was empty except for bales of straw and four automobile tires with rims the boys had stored there.

He climbed back down and went to the house. "There's no one there," he said, "not even one of the cats."

"Robert," Becky said, "she's back. She came back and she's in the barn."

The family decided that none of them would work in the barn alone. The minister who performed the exorcism had moved to another pastorate. They talked of contacting one of the psychics, but except for the footsteps, most of the events could be rationalized. Domestic animals are often panicked by unfamiliar sights and sounds. A fox or some other wild creature could have caused the livestock to run out of the barn. Disease and death are normal happenings on a livestock farm. Animals are as susceptible as humans to heart attacks, ulcers and nervous disorders. Mass hysteria is common among domesticated animals. George began to doubt he had heard heavy footsteps.

Although the house and barn remained quiet, Becky saw it as a temporary condition. This time she would act *before* the events took place. She called her sister one evening and asked her to contact her friend, the psychic. The following Sunday, Rose and her husband drove from Missouri to visit the family.

"My friend is working on another case," Rose told Becky. "She wants me to bring back information about what's happening and she'll be over as soon as she can."

Becky told Rose about the livestock's behavior and deaths, the footsteps in the barn and the malfunctioning lights and radio. "We know people will think we're making something out of nothing," she said, "and after our other experiences we read something supernatural into everything that happens. Sometimes I think we *are* just imagining things. Most everything that happened can be explained one way or another, and if they didn't believe what happened in the house, they're not going to believe it about the barn. If it's our imagination, it's strong enough to worry us again. I don't know what caused the stampede, but if the boys hadn't moved fast, they could have been badly hurt, maybe killed."

Rose called Becky Monday night. "Becky," she said. "My friend thinks you may have reason for concern. It's possible there's a presence in your barn, but it may not be the same presence that was in you house. She suggested that you burn any articles you have that pertain to the supernatural. She said to burn them, not just throw them away. You know, things like books or cards or Ouija boards. Burn them all."

"We do have books we bought when our troubles first

began, and we have a hex sign on the front of the barn. We bought the sign when we were on a trip several years ago. I thought a hex was supposed to ward off evil spirits."

"I'm just telling you what she told me, that it was important that you burn anything you have that has anything to do with supernatural beings or incidents."

Robert and Becky burned the few items they had saved from when their troubles began, a deck of fortune telling cards, several books and newspaper clippings. They tore the hex sign from the barn and burned it, too.

Chapter 22

They burned the books and hex sign in the Fall and the remainder of the year passed without incident. Joseph and the girls were working and George was in High School. Becky was alone in the house most of the time, and as months passed with no unusual sights or sounds, she became convinced their problems were finally over.

The psychic visited several times and talked with them on the telephone. It was her opinion that they were rid of the presences and that there would be no more occurrences.

In one of our conferences, Becky said, "Steve, now that it's all over, which one was it?"

"I thought the psychic was convinced there were two, Mrs. Blake and her father."

"Well, there was a man who died while working on that barn, and the little girl who died so young must have played in it. Mrs. Blake's husband died in the house, but he must have spent a lot of time in the barn. I can't help but wonder if one of them will come back."

"Becky," I said. "I think you're borrowing trouble. Everything has been quiet for some time, hasn't it?"

"Yes," she said, "You're probably right, and I hope it stays that way."

The second year after the exorcism arrived with record-low temperatures. Roads were ice-covered and snow filled road side ditches. Many days, the school busses ran late. The driveway and barnyard at Robert and Becky's farm were treacherous walking.

One late afternoon, Becky was preparing the evening meal. It would be another hour before the school bus would let George off at the end of the driveway and another half hour before the others came home. She had turned off the television and was listening to the radio for a weather report. Soft music was playing as she set the table. As she reached into a drawer for silverware, a voice sounded above the music.

"Mother," it said.

Becky shut the drawer and went to the back door. Evidently, George was home early. She was always worried he might slip and fall on the icy driveway. But there was no one at the back door.

She ran to the family-room window and looked out to the

road. The bus wasn't in sight.

She heard the voice again, clearly, a little girl's voice.

"Mother," she said.

She turned off the radio.

The little girl's voice sounded three more times. Each time it calling, "Mother," louder each time.

She sat at the kitchen table and waited for Robert to come home. Her hands were clenched and she was crying.

The house was quiet.

The house and barn remained quiet. There have been no disturbing incidents. But the troubles have not been forgotten. Always, in their minds, is the fear that the noises, the chilling presences may appear again, perhaps when they least expect it.

As I have visited with the family through the years as a friend, a relative and a confidant, I have often thought of the changes I have witnessed in the family and the farm. The farm evolved from a piece of property that one might easily associate with returned beings, to a typical, prosperous-looking modern midwestern farmstead. The corn and beans grow tall and prolific, and cattle and hogs are well fed.

The family has grown from four, frightened children and their bewildered, concerned parents to a prosperous, active, hardworking and successful entity.

But in the serenity of a cool, autumn afternoon, or the creeping quiet of the night, questions come to mind. Are the unwanted inhabitants from another world and another time still there? Did they leave? Does the mother still grieve for her lost little girl? Is she still bitter and full of gaul for what has been done to her home, her blackberry patch? Does she still hate the dogs and the people who destroyed her world as she knew it? Is the old man still trying to fit into a time and place in which he doesn't belong?

Do they still roam the fields, and slip silently into the lengthening shadows in the sweet hay-strewn barn? Do they stand beneath the tree, invisible this time? Or have they retreated to a world now familiar to them? Or will they, when time and events call to them, return?

Only time will answer.

Most tales arrive at a logical conclusion. Characters react to happenings and situations, problems are solved and questions are answered and that's the end of the story.

In this story, the questions remain. Those who shared the story were frightened, but of what were they frightened? What would be their purpose in inventing tales of spirits and appearances? Why did it happen to this particular family? Was it, as the minister believes, a combination of fear and evil?

Whether it was an unexplainable fear, or an unfamiliar evil, or something entirely supernatural, if it happened to this family, it could, without a doubt, happen to any family.

Watch for other mysteries by Mayhaven Publishing

A Byte of Charity (Lance Pearson)

An Honorable Spy (Warren Carrier)

And Then She Was Gone (Susan McBride)*

Beijing Odyssey (Steve Au)

Ho-Nikon (G. McLeod)

Murder at the Strawberry Festival (Warren Carrier)

No Man's a Mountain (John Cramer)

Waltz With the Devil (Paul Fouliard)

*Mayhaven Award Winner—in its second printing